Psychological Précipice

The Psychological Pursuit To Find The Best In You

Dr. Lawana Rene' Lofton

iUniverse, Inc.
New York   Bloomington

Psychological Précipice
The Psychological Pursuit To Find The Best In You

iUniverse books may be ordered through booksellers or by contacting:

iUniverse
1663 Liberty Drive
Bloomington, IN 47403
www.iuniverse.com
1-800-Authors (1-800-288-4677)

Because of the dynamic nature of the Internet, any Web addresses or links contained in this book may have changed since publication and may no longer be valid. The views expressed in this work are solely those of the author and do not necessarily reflect the views of the publisher, and the publisher hereby disclaims any responsibility for them.

ISBN: 978-1-4401-3057-1 (pbk)
ISBN: 978-1-4401-3059-5 (cloth)
ISBN: 978-1-4401-3058-8 (ebk)

Library of Congress Control Number: 2009925389

Printed in the United States of America

iUniverse rev. date: 8/27/2009

Author Biography

Dr. Lawana Rene' Lofton, Psy.D, is recognized as a highly respected and knowledgeable Psychologist, and Consultant. Dr. Lofton holds a doctoral degree in Clinical Psychology with a program emphasis in Couples Therapy, a Masters of Science Degree in Counseling Psychology, and a Bachelors of Science Degree in Business Management. Dr. Lofton's therapeutic strengths lie in her ability to facilitate strategic change based in fostering mature relationship differentiation for individuals and couples.

The author's proverbial road to here began in 1988 actively facilitating Personal Development Retreats internationally. Dr. Lofton has had a unique opportunity to participate in Personal Development Retreats in Okinawa, Japan, Honolulu, Hawaii, San Diego, California, and then in 1996, received certification in Psychodrama and Group Psychotherapy from the Westwood Institute, Los Angeles, California, an internationally recognized center for professional training and education.

In 2003, while working on a multidisciplinary treatment team in an acute psychiatric hospital providing Group Therapy to inpatients, in addition to Family Therapy discharge planning sessions, the full impact interpersonal relationship dynamics contribute to a patient's sense of overall well being became clear. The number of patients who also requested assistance navigating problematic interpersonal relationships was most surprising given their primary Mental Health crisis warranting hospitalization. Based on human nature, one's ability to surpass an individual personal crisis is adaptive, yet to sustain it will also require an appropriate level of external management of mature interpersonal relationships with others.

In keeping with a professional commitment to promote the accessibility of strategies a modern day psychological approach can offer, Dr. Lofton established in 2007 a professional consulting practice which offers a venue individuals and couples can obtain information, attend educational seminars, gain support, and resources, all to foster their psychological best. The *Psychological Précipice* in many ways is an accumulation of professional knowledge Dr. Lofton has gained thus far in the practice of Clinical Psychology on how human nature contributes to, and limits, an individual's innate ability to live a fulfilling and extraordinary life.

The author's inspiration for writing this book is motivated by the need to contribute to the discussion on what constitutes *Psychological Normalcy* in a modern society. Furthermore, the main intent is to assist individuals and couples in their pursuit to learn how to bring out the best in them regardless of their present life dilemmas, or difficulties. To be *Psychologically Normal* is a common expression we all take liberty with, yet remains not well elaborated upon given it is human nature to encounter significant stressors throughout the developmental life span. Everyone would consider himself or herself normal and well adjusted, until they begin to discuss how they navigate interpersonal relationships. The domain of sustaining appropriate and mature relationships appears to stand out as an area of grave dysfunction even among our most adjusted in society, and because of this, warrants further investigation and discussion.

Lastly, in the field of Psychology, given its vast evolutionary intellectual adaptations to advance, remains stagnant. In a modern day society the field of Psychology proceeded only by its ability to include the advances made within scientific neurological brain imaging technology, the field of psychological practice has remained one of intellectual consolidation and refinement as we have seen in years prior when the physics of science was at its infancy. It is the author's hope the general public, Psychologists, Psychiatrists, Medical & Health Care Professionals, Couples Therapist, Sex Therapists, and the broader helping professions, discover distinctive nuances of empowerment crucial today for understanding, facilitating, and effecting change with those they seek to help.

Dedication

To *Mankind,* that part in each of us, who continues to wonder regardless of gender or social influence. This part, which remains curious of their present state, and of the possibilities, which exist in the pursuit to create a compelling future.

So often in life we create for ourselves determined boundaries so carefully crafted, yet effortlessly can be deconstructed with only the slightest touch of innovation and one person's willingness to initiate it. When change is needed, it is not good enough to just see the need for change, but someone to take the lead in executing it painstakingly through resistance, and to completion. With any great need for change, in a social construct, the decision to pursue a meaningful relationship or to pursue a personal endeavor to give life meaning, the challenges will always include components of curiosity, initiative, and implementation.

Contents

PART I:

PSYCHOLOGICAL FOUNDATIONS

CHAPTER ONE

Intellectual Adaptation

*P*eople are basically good and capable of sustaining all they aspire to become. The author wishes not to call what the role of a Psychologist sets out to achieve with its patients as solely a facilitating agent for change, but rather Psychologist are often placed in a unique vantage point to offer their patients opportunities to explore new insights about themselves. To explore a patient's current motivation level for change and beyond this, a great Psychologist allows patients the time and space to examine decisively their current life dilemma *if* the patient deems it necessary to do so.

Coaxing, manipulating, or encouraging a forced change in patients should never be a misappropriated role of what a professional Psychologist sets out to do with patients. Rather, perhaps perfect in our patients more fully who they already are. Then, the patient fueled with a new perspective on their unique life dilemmas, can then decide to take greater responsibility for the direction of their life.

What we as a society have come to call Modern Day Clinical Psychology Practices is accessible to everyone, yet unfortunately as a society; we continue to associate its benefits as only reserved for the Mentally Ill in North America. Or, the fundamental core benefits of what Psychology has to offer those in society is repackaged under the guise of Self Help and is then utilized by the masses after this repackaging effect has carefully removed all traces of a perceived attached social stigma. It is this author's contention that Modern Day Clinical Psychology's benefits is relevant for everyone if we as professionals in the field of Psychology can take decisive actions towards greater inclusion of research topics within the field. In a time of Modern Psychology where it would appear, all the great discoveries have already occurred, have been intellectually consolidated into other theories or refined, there remains room for a novel discovery.

The focus of this book will offer a new approach to Psychology in making its concepts more accessible, highlighting an individual's strengths over weaknesses' which has so largely been the focus in Psychology. The framework for this text will explore not only where Psychology evolved from, but where the focus on a new approach to viewing the benefits of Psychology will bring about the greatest impact for those who elect to learn more about the application of Psychology into daily living. It is the study of an evolving Psychology.

My personal history within the field of Psychology commenced in 1988 and has ultimately brought me to a place presently where it can be stated in all honesty Psychology remains a new frontier open for exploration, expansion, and a platform to advocate for broader research topics which will ultimately be for the betterment of all. Regardless of an individual's chosen line of work within the broad profession of Mental Health Care and Psychiatric Services, contributing to the debate in one's field benefits all ultimately.

Lastly, the author will challenge preconceived notions of Psychological Normalcy, and ultimately present a compelling argument as to why the pursuit of quality relationships is crucial to one's overall Psychological Growth.

A Brief History of Philosophy

Philosophy is the love of *knowledge*. It can be described as an agreed upon platform from which concepts and ideas can be explained and interpreted. Popular themes in Philosophy include Critical Thinking, Logic, Ethics, Aesthetics, Metaphysics, and Epistemology. The *knowledge* one stands to gain from studying Philosophy can take us to despair as we contemplate concepts of Nihilism outlined in 1875 by German Philosopher Friedrich Nietzsche. Nihilism being the belief that states *nothing* in life is worthwhile as there is no objective basis for truth. Alternatively, in ones pursuit to gain *knowledge* through understanding the basis from which Philosophy formed, a person can achieve a new sense of empowerment through the incremental exposure to varying perspectives which exist to interpret the human condition and concepts that have explained what gives life ultimate meaning.

The relationship between Philosophy and Psychology are interrelated. Psychology, as a professional discipline of study, evolved from Philosophy to continue examining beliefs and concepts Philosophy attempts to clarify for society. In Philosophy, questions considered paramount at its creation in 600 BC, focused on explaining what motivated the development of the universe. Early Philosophers formulated theories considered significant because they allowed a structure to make sense of the otherwise unexplainable. Theories provide a foundation from which individuals can then make predictions for not only society as a whole to lessen uncertainty, but also in making predictions of those individually in society. For instance, if you are a Psychologist and with a patient, we attempt to explain something we have never experienced before.

Psychological theory provides a means to organize material presented by the patient and after the Psychologist has become familiar with the patient and understands more fully the unique life dynamics presented to analyze their presenting problem, the patient becomes more human, and the theory seamlessly fades into the background. The theory remains the overwriting foundation from which to conceptualize a presenting problem, in addition to instilling a degree of certainty for the Psychologist that they can then compare future insights against for perspective.

In Philosophy, there continue to be perplexing questions, which remain unanswered as they have centuries past to include what changes and what remains the same over time. Why is there competing forces like love and hate? Why is it humans are capable of so much good and are capable of so much hate? Philosophers continue to question who we are as a human race and how we evolved. What is the meaning of life? Is there a God? Do us, as humans need to believe in one God or more than one God to explain the nature of existence. Many in society would argue God comes in many forms, while some do not believe in a God at all. Primary questions, which remain pivotal in Modern Psychology, are if people are inherently good. How can people attain happiness? What motives or drives do people have? Are human beings naturally social?

A brief investigation into the history of Philosophy and Psychology can assist readers discover what truly motivates individual conduct, and to understand our collective innate desire to seek fulfillment in a Modern Society.

For the intellectually curious, it is important to review existing patterns in the literature, which resurface over time to have an appreciation for the depth and scope of advances made in Modern Psychology as well as existing limitations. Many fundamental core concepts first described in Greek Philosophical literature, have been transformed into new concepts for a Modern Psychology, but are not in actuality novel in part, just well established historical concepts elaborated upon further for a new time frame. Furthermore, all concepts from the past that have successfully stood the test of time are not necessarily true, nor is it so that those which did not survive historical time lines were necessarily inaccurate in their intent and scope. Geography, individual success gained in publishing efforts, and civil environmental factors, have all influenced significantly societal perspectives based on what literary content continues to be perpetuated in the literature, and what is not.

The first Philosophers in 600 BC were Thales, Anaximander, and Anaximenes. Thales was the first to introduce themes of mythology to explain what was occurring in the universe along with measuring the pyramids, studying Geometry, and Astronomy. In 600 BC, the focus remained on understanding the nature of the universe specifically how the universe formed. Greek Athenian Philosophers of the 4th and 3rd BC shifted their focus wherein many became concerned with civil unrest and individual insecurity in Athens. Philosophers then became concerned with problems of the individual so they began to focus on Ethics to help individuals achieve tranquility in a period of change when things seemed out of control due to the effects of war. Early Philosophers taught people not to fear the unknown, namely death. This was an important discussion for early Philosophers as it remained pure speculation, or based on supernatural suspicions prevalent, to explain what occurred after death. These questions more importantly sparked a debate as to whether the concept of a soul separate from one's physical structure existed or not.

Socrates

Socrates, an Athenian Greek (469 – 399 BC), wrote no Philosophical writings, but was uniquely influential on his students and followers also of Greek decent, Plato, Aristotle, Aristippus, and Antisthenes. The Philosophy of Socrates has been extracted from manuscripts documented later through the writings by Plato and Aristotle. Socrates' Philosophical interests were Epistemology, Ethics, and on the conduct of life. Socrates was convinced that our souls were the development and of the acting upon of virtues and vices, considered more important for our individual lives than our bodies, or external circumstances encountered.

He also believed he had been singled out by the Gods because he was aware of what he did not know, and could appreciate his limitations. Socrates' greatest accomplishment is being known for the development of the Socratic Method used in Law School, which is the use of questions to get students to think critically. Socrates was by all accounts a minimalist and was committed to leading a simplistic life style.

In Philosophy, the term Epistemology is a phrase commonly used to describe the viewpoints expressed that addresses theories of *knowledge.* Epistemology is concerned with the definition of *knowledge,* its sources, the criteria used to describe *knowledge,* as well as the degree in which *we* can be certain regarding the validity of *knowledge* gained and its limitations. Epistemology is a course of study that challenges an individual's intellectual sense of reason and deductive reasoning abilities of finding truth as well as what forces in life we are limited by as humans. The way we view and experience the world evolves overtime based on what we collectively accept as *knowledge,* which is partly a split between one's unique set of individual beliefs, and what the individual believes is *true* for them.

Materialism Versus Dualism

Materialism: Epicurus and Hippocrates

The quintessential need to understand human nature led early Philosophers to investigate how humans think. Even today, this basic question continues to be deliberated in both Psychological, Philosophical literature, and among scholars who study Ethics. The basic urge to understand the efficiency of *how* behavior occurs as referred to in Modern Psychology as Behaviorism, and the purpose or *why* humans do what they do, would later be adapted, and elaborated upon further in Sigmund Freud's theories on Psychoanalytical Psychology, which all speak to the inquiries of early Philosophers.

This line of thought led Philosophers to question if they individually believed there was something that continued to exist outside the body, even after death. Subsequently two schools of thought emerged with opposing beliefs regarding the basic components that make up human nature. Those who considered the body, comprised only of a physical structure as the source of what makes humans what they are, are referred to as Materialist. Materialism contends all mental activity is due to activity of a physical system comprised of matter, or purely atoms. A physical substance of atoms and all phenomena is the result of material interactions. Those who focused on how the soul combined with the physical structure to explain human nature became established as a Dualist Theory. Dualism advocated that human beings possess both, a physical structure and a separate component referred to as a soul. Reportedly, the body may operate according to the rules of the physical universe, but the soul was considered a non-physical entity that exists on a spiritual plane subject to different principles.

In Epicurean Materialism Philosophy, Epicurus believed individuals "like everything else, is composed of atoms. The term "soul" is used by Epicurus to indicate the activity of those atoms responsible for cognition and other mental phenomena" (Scavio & Regas, 1997). To describe human nature, Epicurus' perspective is considered mechanistic, yet thorough and clear. Epicurus explained the individual thought process, feelings, mindfulness, and what constitutes individual will, are the result of a thought process influenced only by ones physical structure. The Epicurean perspective helped to lower and contain society's misperceptions regarding supernatural concepts, and prevailing concepts of the time not easily defined nor explained scientifically regarding the existence of a soul as defined in Dualism. Epicurus theory contends that by learning the nature of the universe and of death, removes fear of the supernatural considered the worst form of mental pain.

According to an Epicurean Materialism Theory, human nature is constructed of matter namely atoms and in death, like all other substances including the concept of a soul, the atoms of the soul dissipate into the void of the universe. Based on Epicurus' premise that life is not infinite and in death nothing remains, he encouraged his students to ponder if this was true, then ethically, how should humans conduct their lives if they have but one life to live? The pursuit of mental fulfillment, the use of discretion, and limiting desire will maximize both longevity and happiness Epicurean Materialism asserted. A popular term associated with Epicurean Materialism Theory is the Latin term *eudemonia via ataraxia,* translated means *happiness through mental tranquility* (Hibler, 1984; Scavio & Regas, 1997). The term *ataraxia* is also referenced in the literature to mean limiting mental disturbances, such as excessive worry and conflicts found in everyday existence. Additionally, the use of restraint in seeking pleasure and the use of denial were also advocated. Based on what has evolved in Modern Psychology, we know it is instinctual for humans to exercise varying degrees of denial, but is it ever warranted or good to do so. Is it ever healthy or a precursor to achieving a means towards securing long-term happiness?

Contemplating reality too much can lead to unhappiness according to Philosopher Pyrrho (360 - 270 BC), yet Epicurus believed understanding the nuances of the universe fosters happiness understandably because it would dispel any fears connected to fears of the unknown. Adapted, and further examined in the literature we discover in later 1875 Nietzsche's theories of Nihilism with a similar agreement with Pyrrho.

We say that pleasure is the beginning and end of living happily.

Epicurus' Moral Theory

Both Plato and Aristotle in their collective Philosophies questioned the fundamental principles of happiness also found in Epicurean Materialism Theories. According to Epicurus, humans seek pleasure. In doing so, disrupts the natural state of being human. The highest forms of pleasure are intellectual pursuits, not physical nor through sensual erotic means, he clarified. Hence, ultimate pleasure occurs when the mind is free of anguish, anxiety, and strong desires.

He explained through his careful description that if pleasure is pursued, it will naturally manifest a disturbance leading to pain, and happiness can only be restored after the individual returns to their natural state. In satisfying one's personal desires will surely manifest feelings of pleasure, and he cautioned as a result some pleasures bring pain in their wake. Therefore, desire should be limited to those desires considered only natural and necessary.

Similar to Epicurean Philosophical Theory, the Pleasure – Pain Principle developed in the 20th Century as a paradigm now associated with Modern Psychological theories of Sigmund Freud, Thorndike, and B. F. Skinner. Moreover, many of the central themes made clear by Epicurus Theory, particularly the tendency of the human condition to feel desire and to limit it, has important implications for Mental Health Diagnostic conditions of Psychopathology, and Personality Disorders. Specific components found in Epicurean Philosophy left unelaborated upon further in his writings is considered to have additional relevance in Modern Psychology. Its applicability today is associated with individual disturbances created if people are not successful in obtaining or navigating their individual needs. A disturbance in ones mental processes is created that contributes to difficulty sustaining one's natural state of homeostasis. This can all too easily perpetuate other conflicts found in associated areas of basic daily functioning.

Hippocrates (460-370 BC) of Greek decedent, considered the founder of modern medicine, believed one's bodily fluids could determine an individual's overall physical health, human temperament, personality, and mood. Hippocrates taught medicine and compiled patient case histories with detailed observations on the course of diseases. Hippocrates is one of the first scholars to challenge the notion that disease was *not* a punishment sent from the Gods. He believed that all illnesses, including Mental Illnesses, had natural origins. Many of Hippocrates theories on Materialism have proved accurate over the centuries specifically his assertions that brain dysfunction was considered to be the source of the most serious diseases and responsible for psychological disorders.

Dualism: Plato and Aristotle

Both Plato and Aristotle were Dualist believing that a physical structure, and an *entity* referred to as a soul comprised human nature. According to Plato, absolute truth exists independent of the physical body. He speculated that an *entity* existed beyond the assertions made by Hippocrates' theories of physical health to explain the totality of how humans obtain truth and *knowledge*. Plato speculated ones senses help us to discover the innate forms which already exist. According to Plato's Rationalism Theory[1f], humans are excited by their senses, and then ones intellect becomes stimulated allowing humans to think of the *knowledge* built inside of us, innate, with which we are born with. In 387 BC, Plato suggested that the brain is the mechanism of mental processes, further supporting his conviction to Christianity, believing that *knowledge* was fixed and can be discovered through introspection. By 335 BC, Aristotle, suggested that the heart was the mechanism of mental processes in contrast.

Plato stated ones true nature could be known through the human mind that he explained in his concept called *Forms*. Plato's conceptualized theories were not conveyed straightforwardly; therefore, the reader is required to extract Plato's meaning through analyzing his stories. Plato's many manuscripts all have deep meaning for the curious thinker. Perhaps of all Plato's writings and accomplishments considered most noteworthy is Plato's role in establishing *The Academy* for higher learning, along with several writings he completed including his *Dialogues; The Symposium*, and *The Republic* in which he wrote *The Allegory Of The Cave.*

The Allegory Of The Cave is a story of people who live in a cave. The story makes the connection that living in a material world, a modern society we as humans experience physically, is comparable to living in a cave sheltered from the realities of life. As the story is depicted, the inhabits of the cave can see glimpses of shadows that come into the cave either through the light that comes into the cave naturally, or through the light that the inhabitants of the cave make with fire.

---

1 f Rationalism is a naturalistic alternative to appeals of religious accounts of human nature and conduct. More specifically, rationalism is the epistemological theory that significant knowledge of the world can best be achieved by *a priori* means; it therefore stands in contrast to empiricism. Prominent rationalists of the modern period include *Descartes, Spinoza*, and *Leibniz.*

Inhabits of the cave can only see shadows on the wall, and they think those shadows reflect something ideal and perfect. If the inhabits of the cave were to walk out of the cave and into the bright sunlight of the unsheltered world, those in the cave could see the true beauty that is. A true depiction of what reality is. We assume the shadows are perfect, but if we walked out into the sunlight we could see how beautiful things are in their natural form, unfiltered, but because once outside of the cave people become so flooded, blinded from the sunlight, or over stimulated, they retreat back into the comfort of the cave they have become so use to. Back into the cave most would go and pretend what they are seeing is ideal.

Plato in his writings was attempting to convey that *Man* is attempting to reunite with the non-material unsheltered and unfiltered ideal world, but we settle. We settle for the pale shadows. We all want to be vulnerable and we want to be protected at the same time as we may become overwhelmed if ever faced with the true meaning of life. The core meaning of life, and how to adapt it to one's existence.

There is deeper meaning, but the interpretation this author has come to deduct from his writings as well as many others have deducted from his *Dialogue The Allegory Of The Cave,* is that Plato speculated societies efforts of *adapting to truth,* that which can be revealed by existing in a life unfiltered by the shadows reflected in the cave, is through love. Meaning, the living of ones life authentically and genuinely unfiltered by obstructions a cave can provide. Love is the transforming experience to become reunited with the ideal of an unsheltered world. This may have been why Plato placed so much importance on concepts of goodness and beauty in his literature.

The *Allegory Of The Cave* depicts ordinary humanity as so shackled by illusions several times removed from the illumination of truth that only radical moral and intellectual conversion could redeem them. Plato's theories also address the human psyche as being in conflict with opposing desires to use reason and resisting the desire to succumb to one's emotions. In the absence of personal accountability when internal conflicts surface, Plato speculated characterizes a moral disease.

Plato provided additional concepts for the reader to consider through his writings in which he titled *Forms* to explain truth, and his beliefs regarding the existence of God in forms and ideas apart from reality. The concepts he explained in *Forms* are associated to a physical world we encounter here on earth, where life is always changing, in contrast to the spiritual world where things remain the same. His writing on *Forms* outline a basic understanding of three concepts he termed, *Beauty*, *Truth*, and *Goodness*. Plato believed absolute truth exists independent of the physical world on earth for humans. In the spiritual world, there are *Forms* and undisputable truths, which remain the same over time. The mind can ascertain these absolute ideas, or unchallengeable truths, through a process we can initiate and experience here on earth by understanding *Forms* of *Beauty, Truth, and Goodness.*

Forms

Beauty

The first concept is *Beauty* and is first on the list, placed at the lowest level of the hierarchy. An example of this would be admiring another person's physical beauty, the perfection of a beautiful flower, or admiring a work of art one considers beautiful. It is the easiest form for humans to see. It is the physical beauty in appearance. It is the physical beauty one can see in another or in objects considered aesthetically beautiful or pleasing to the eye.

Truth

Truth can be seen in *knowledge.* If we work hard enough, we could get to undisputable truth. Mathematics and Science attempt to give us factual truth.

Goodness

Goodness is the highest form of ideal types that were immutable our society has put above all others Plato wrote. Plato speculated that a soul is necessary to explain how *Man* comes to know something from the non-material world. There would have to be a non-material entity, a soul connected to us, to make it possible to make sense of the non-material. *Man's* confusion then comes from assuming what happens in the material world is an accurate reflection of reality. The physical objects we see are several steps removed from *Man* and he cannot make sense of a non-material world with a physical body. Plato further contended that *Man's* confusion in life comes from assuming that the physical objects we can make sense of in everyday living; life as it were, is *life* as it was meant to be lived in an ideal form. Meaning life exists in the physical world as much as it can be reflected and understood several steps removed from its actual ideal form.

For example, in physical narcissism a person may attempt to make themselves into something perfect. People then start to believe they are perfect. Our society is not perfect, nor above the world, but can come to believe our actions, physical appearance, and decisions we make as a whole are ideal and perfect, and over time translate this into an acceptable degree of truth. History teaches us we never find absolute truth, we just come close.

Several variations made upon Plato's theme of *Forms* are found in popular literature in various cultures around the globe. One variation is a story told in China written of a vagrant who enters a temple to shelter himself from the rain. As the story is told, the vagrant's life is void of moral decisions and to make ends meet over the years has taken other's possession in society to support himself financially. While taking refuge from the elements inside the temple, he discovers an abandoned newborn. Unable to find anyone who would care for the newborn the vagrant is then forced to take responsibility for the newborn and becomes transformed by his new responsibilities. The vagrant experiences love for the first time due to his act of goodness.

Another variation to Plato's theme of *Forms,* published in Japan, depicts a migrant female who profits off the dead in adverse times. In the short story titled *Rashomon* (Akutagawa, 1952), a Japanese servant to a samurai we discover as the story unfolds is newly terminated from his position due to effects of a rapidly declining economy. Coincidently, as in the previous version on *Forms* depicted above, an abandoned ancient temple is used in this story as well as the backdrop in the story and used to metaphorically provide shelter from the elements both real and spiritual.

Earthquakes, fire, calamities, and hardship have devastated the city of Kyoto, in which the servant resides. Many over the years have been affected and to an almost ironic ending, there sits the servant at the steps of a ancient temple now known for being a place to dispose of unclaimed corpses. A seemly metaphorical end of the road as well.

Newly terminated, the servant seeks refuge from the chill of the night's wind and rain on the abandoned temple's steps. He contemplates the weight of his new employment status. Feelings of hopelessness quickly become his focus and cloud his perspective as he contemplates what may lie ahead given the unforeseen devastation in the city. The servant considers his state of homelessness, and limited options. More importantly, he must conjure up an inner wherewithal to create a compelling future for himself to survive. In this moment of reflective solitude to confront his horrifying state, he considers becoming a thief as a means of finding economic support. The decision he makes goes against his sense of honor in comparison to the previous role he held as a trusted servant to the samurai.

> *He had little choice of means, whether fair or foul, because of his helpless circumstances. If he chose honest means, he would undoubtedly starve to death besides the wall or in the Sujaku gutter.*
>
> *Akutagawa, 1970*

Reason enters his thought process and thoughts of consequences, yet in light of his limited compelling options he was perplexed as to what to do next. Basic needs of survival enter his thought process clouding all reason and logic of how one must proceed in moments of doubt.

Although the smell of corpses in the temple is offensive, he enters the temple to sleep. There he finds a woman he does not know and he bares witness to her pulling the hair out of the dead. He questions her actions and she responds, "It is to make a wig to sale at market."

> *He did not know if whether her case was to be put down as good or bad. But in his eyes, pulling the hair of the dead in the Rashomon on this stormy night was a unpardonable crime. Of course it never entered his mind that a little while ago he had thought of becoming a thief.*
>
> *Akutagawa, 1970*

He had little choice of means whether fair or foul, because of his seemingly hopeless circumstances. If he chose honest means, he would undoubtedly starve to death. The moment man contemplates veering from what has been their basis for forming a fundamental character base; it begs the question is man decent? Do we lie to protect ourselves from the lies and behaviors we do to others?

Philosophy has answered for all of *Mankind* many questions. Yet, questions remain. Inside us all individually if given the time and space for honest reflection on one's intentions, discord remains as well for the masses.

Philosophy perhaps can only describe the general nuances discovered within the field of study based on what has come before, and then individually *Mankind* must come to their own conclusions based on unique circumstances they encounter that challenges one's current understanding of truth and of their character they wish to preserve in life. People hold the truth for themselves, not an over riding regurgitated conceptualization that has yet to be articulated by those in society. We have it inside of us all.

Aristotle

In 400 BC, Aristotle was first to document concepts and discoveries on scientific observation, abstraction, and of Science in his Dualism Theory of Materialism. Aristotle unlike Plato's Rationalistic interpretation of the mind, Aristotle developed Dualism incorporating an empirical formula. Aristotle is credited for developing what is known today as Hypothesis Testing and Scientific Methods. He is known for believing that *knowledge* is acquired after birth, and then is expanded upon over time in contrast to Plato's belief all knowledge is innate. The perspective of Aristotle holds all *knowledge* is accumulated over time using empirical methods supported by the use of scientific methods. From this perspective, Modern Psychology has adapted similar themes and terms to include *The Blank Slate Theory*. Aristotle was a student of Plato then later became his adversary developing different ideas. This form of literary discord on how to best interrupt a certain intellectual idea is not new, nor considered negative. In retrospect, is considered acceptable in order that *knowledge* can be elaborated upon further, corrected, or merely explained from a different vantage point. Sigmund Freud for example had students who would take his theories, and then take then into another direction like Freud's daughter Anna. Or, Melanie Kline who took some theory based liberties from the work developed by Carl Jung.

Aristotle stated all *knowledge* is acquired through experience. Many scholars believe Aristotle's development of Empiricism is the initial most comprehensive foundation for the Birth of Science and a worthy marker for the Beginning of Psychology. It would not be until 1800 Wilhelm Wundt received official credit for establishing Experimental Psychology and is now considered by most to be the beginning of Modern Psychology.

Aristotle relied on giving lectures to students and considered a tutor to Alexander the Great. Because of their friendship, Alexander provided financial funding which allowed Aristotle to establish the School Lyceum to study Zoology and Biology. Aristotle contributed to the biological sciences and to the development of Scientific Methods. He believed objects change constantly, but it was due to an unscientific divine intervention.

The core foundations we now consider classical perspectives found in Philosophy originated in Athens, Greece, prior to 500 AD. After 500 AD, a period formed giving rise to what is referred to as The Dark Ages whereby Athens was devastated by the effects of war and subsequent foreign occupations. Rome, excreted power and influence over much of Western and Eastern Europe including Athens under the guise of an occupation called The Byzantine Empire. The Byzantine Empire was considered an extension of Rome and of its Eastern Europe occupation in Constantinople; its physical location is now Istanbul, Turkey. Those who comprised the Byzantine Empire spoke Greek, Latin, Coptic, Syriac, and Armenian. During the Byzantine period, many of Athens' artwork including its literature on Philosophy were moved to Constantinople, and the temples in Athens became Christian churches.

With the fall of Rome however, by 1453 AD, the Roman Empire was defeated by the Ottoman Turkish. In some contexts, the Ottoman Turks were considered Muslim, relating to a classical stage of civilization in archaic Greece that is no longer accurate. The period between 634 - 642 BC, Arabians inspired by a new religion known as Islam, conquered Palestine, Syria, Mesopotamia, and Egypt. By 1458, the Ottoman Turkish gained complete control of Athens whereby they transformed the Parthenon in Athens into a Muslim mosque. Artwork and Philosophical literature then held in Constantinople would later become the property of the Ottoman Turkish as they gained control over Constantinople as well. Real keepers of classical literature is believed to have changed ownership, original manuscripts although sparse in quantity are believed to have been maintained and preserved, but in the language of those who held them including the lion's share of knowledge originated by Greek Philosophers. After the fall of Rome, the Muslims retained the majority of the Philosophical and Scientific quantities of *knowledge*, and then the Western Universities developed. The later translations and efforts to distribute the content of Philosophy manuscripts held would make it possible for a larger global audience to benefit from original Greek Philosophy.

The Compromise

After the Roman Empire fell, church authority rules, specifically the Roman Catholic Church's establishment of a hierarchy of *knowledge,* persisted. Few were willing to challenge the order of the day, yet many were focused on challenging Aristotle's earlier assertions that knowledge was not innate and was acquired through out ones life capable of abstract thinking using both one's mind to establish intellect and a soul. Subsequently, contemporary religion scholars began interrupting Philosophy and concluded that how humans come to acquire *knowledge* must come from a spiritual non-material origin, and Philosophy was best suited to address some matters that would also include matters of understanding religion. A second major division occurred among scholars wherein arguments surfaced to dispute religious faith based facts, compared to what Science could conclude based on reason. St. Thomas Aquinas, an Italian Catholic Theologian, Professor, and Philosopher, in the 13th Century, stated if ever there was a conflict between choosing faith over reasoning found in Science, individuals should choose faith because humans are fallible in their thinking. He agreed with Aristotle's beliefs senses stimulate the mind and is continued in the soul.

If humans acquire their ability to think and use deductive reasoning known as intelligence from both the expansive void of the universe originated by a supreme being namely God, and intelligence is influenced by a physical structure called the mind, scholars of the time stated firmly this would defy the Laws of Physics. Therefore, to resolve competing arguments there became a pressing need for agreement or further investigation to determine which perspective was indeed factual. Rene Descartes in response proposed a Cartesian Compromise [2f] that would allow for a safe alternative among faithful and Empiricist could all agree on. Descartes' theory states God created truth and held the belief the soul related to the brain through the *pineal*

---

2   f Cartesian Compromise proposed by Rene Descartes attempted to combine Rationalism, the view point that knowledge is based on sense experience as in divine revelation, opposed to Empiricism in which experience is the source of ideas, reason, observation, and the use of scientific methods, to acquire knowledge.

gland [3f] located within the brain. He speculated because physical structures distort our understanding of the world ones senses are important so only Rationalism can correct what the brain cannot sensor. Up until this period, Science and Philosophy were used jointly to investigate if a soul existed and how it contributes to obtaining new *knowledge*. The Cartesian Compromise brought about the separation to neutralize conflicts against an established faith based hierarchy of *knowledge* and subsequently created greater conflict in the form of greater volumes of invalid information. The establishment of precedence was set. The quest to establish ultimate truth in *knowledge* has the right to be challenged, and the existence of validity and agreement will continue to play a greater role over acceptance.

17th Century Insanity As a Medical Concern

The Bethlem Royal Hospital, London, is considered the first Psychiatric Hospital. The facility in 1247 was a monastery, and then in 1330 was certified as a hospital. In 1403, the Mentally Ill were admitted. The Mentally Ill during this time were considered immorally criminal, social outcasts, or experienced difficulty remaining hidden in society. So when they were discovered, they were promptly confined.

In the 17th Century, the *Places of Confinement* for the Mentally Ill in Europe increased and with it came an increasing demand for Psychiatric Hospitals, employment opportunities to fill the vacancies of Psychiatric Attendants, Medical Supervisors, and the birth of Psychiatry was established. Psychiatry became the medical specialty developing and organizing during the time specifically to address a new medical phenomenon growing termed Mental Disorders (Lofton, 2004). During this century, individual medical physicians committed themselves to the care of the Mentally Ill and published written manuscripts about Mental Insanity.

---

3   f The pineal gland is a cone shaped glad behind the thalamus located in the brain responsible for regulating the body's internal clock and daily circadian rhythms. When signaled by the hypothalamus, the pineal secretes the hormone melatonin. Melatonin is the hormone that regulates sleep and wakefulness. Its levels rise at night and falls during the day. Melatonin has also in recent years been researched with data concluding in support melatonin significantly impacts the immune system if proper levels are not maintained.

The Medical, Philosophical, and literary writings on insanity were often impossible to differentiate. Consequently, determining who was actually insane, immorally criminal, and who would be more justly classified into a category of social inappropriateness, or socially undesirable, played a role in the public's acceptance of mental insanity as a medical concern.

It was believed that the contributions of these early Psychiatrists made no more significant progress than those who had tried to cure the Mentally Ill before them (Lofton, 2004). Notwithstanding, when you factor in the European time period and social agreements made to isolate and punish those in society who for whatever civil, infliction of disease, or environmental factors occurring in the economy which precluded them from caring for themselves, a organized mechanism of confinement was viewed as a viable option.

Psychiatric Hospitals by the 18th Century quickly became known for cruel treatment of the Mentally Ill as well as marking a period in which Mental Illness become perceived as a medical disease to be diagnosed and potentially cured. By 1774, Franz Mesmer detailed his cure for some Mental Illnesses. By 1784, The Narrenturm Hospital, Vienna, was built specifically to admit the Mentally Ill and marked a substantial precedence in history to meet the need of a growing population of people in need of care.

In 1793, French Physician and pioneer in Psychiatry, Philippe Pinel, is credited for advocating the humane treatment of Mentally Ill patients as well as initial efforts to classify mental disorders. French Philosopher Michel Foucault references the Paris, France, Bicêtre Hospital, where Pinel was a Superintendent, in his book titled *The Birth of the Asylum* from Foucault's *Madness and Civilization* series. In it, Foucault depicts Pinel's efforts as more devious than humane. The Philosopher Foucault is also credited for making an astute connection between societies need to confine and punish the socially inapt, criminally inclined, and the need to confine the Mentally Ill.

British Philosopher Thomas Hobbs renews the cause for Materialism. He believed all knowledge comes from experiences. Additionally, the human potential for treachery and self-destructiveness may prove in fact to be innate as described in earlier accounts found throughout classical Philosophy. British Empiricism born from the Materialism of Hobbes he explained was to be a victim of the Materialism [4f] offered by Darwinism. Herbert Spenser stated the evolution of mental abilities is tied to the evolution of the brain and applied Darwinism to Psychology and Socialism. Charles Darwin published *On the Origin of Species (1859)*, detailing his view of evolution and on the theory "Survival Of The Fittest" by Herbert Spenser. A statement of differentiation within a species resulting in sexual selection allowing the fittest to procreate. Social Darwinism is the perspective we must ensure freedom in society by allowing the fittest among us to survive by allowing the weak in society to die out because it promoted a better society. Whether we agree with Social Darwinism or not this viewpoint has perhaps historically influenced society's perspective as to how best to provide confinement and treatment of the Mentally Ill. Or, more accurately, care for those so devastated by their experiences and natural tendency to be both good, criminal, socially inappropriate.

By 1861, a third shift occurred wherein Scientific Methods appeared to take a greater role affecting both biological and neurological anatomy research for a developing scientific Psychology. French physician Paul Broca discovered an area in the left frontal lobe of the brain key to language development. Sir Francis Galton in 1869, influenced by Charles Darwin's *Origin Of The Species*, published *Hereditary Genius* and argued intellectual abilities were biological in nature. He also developed Statistics considered the staple Psychologist's use to interrupt Psychological research results. By 1874, Carl Wernicke, a German Psychiatrist and Neurologist, was successful in publishing his research on the posterior temporal lobe of the left hemisphere of the brain responsible for receptive speech.

---

4 [f] Materialism is the belief that only physical things exist. Materialists state every mental phenomenon is a result of a physical object. Classical Materialists include Hobbes, and La Mettrie.

Pragmatism According To Charles Peirce

Society, it would seem, now influenced by the results a calculated scientific approach can have, wanted something concrete, well founded, testable it could use as a instrument tool. Historically, scholars attempted to make descriptions of reality, and then tried to make it fit an established, well-accepted form of reality, or truth in *knowledge*.

Charles Peirce, American Philosopher, is the founder of Pragmatism. Despite his significant contributions, Charles Peirce did not receive full recognition deserving for the contributions he made. This is mostly attributed to the fact many of Peirce's manuscripts were considered incomplete or fragmented. He also had a broad interest of study with more emphasis placed on Mathematics, Astronomy, Logic, and Science vice a sole focus of furthering Philosophy through completing manuscripts focused on Logic.

Charles Peirce influenced William James, American Philosopher, who published *Principles of Psychology*, which would later become the foundation for Functionalism in 1890. William James regarded two of Charles Peirce's published papers, *The Fixation of Belief* (1877), and *How to Make Our Ideas Clear* (1878), as Pragmatism's origin. Pragmatism asserts that ideas are only useful if they help a person adapt to their environment. According to William James, he explains Pragmatism is a theory of truth attempting to make clear what is agreement; the belief is true if it agrees with reality. Or, our collective understanding of reality.

How we can approach concepts of truth with wonder, as well as examining claims based on preconceived notions of logic, Charles Pierce states all knowledge can be mistaken based on a concept he termed Falibilism[5f]. Peirce outlined a structure for examining truth and the use of logical deductive reasoning to make things clear. His theories, at first glance, appear to be circular reasoning. The use of inferring, questioning, the importance of having a preconceived object of ideas, or beliefs first in order to relate it to something

---

5 f Fallibilism is the philosophical doctrine that all claims of knowledge could, in principle, be mistaken. Some Fallibilists go further, arguing that absolute certainty about knowledge is impossible. As a formal doctrine, it is most strongly associated with Charles Sanders Peirce, John Dewey, and other pragmatists, who use it in their attacks on foundationalism. However, it is arguably already present in the views of some ancient philosophers, including Xenophanes, Socrates, and Plato.

else, and upon which to question our ideas or beliefs against. Charles Peirce wrote the one unpardonable offense as a philosophical barricade against truth's advance, an offense to which metaphysicians in all ages have shown themselves the most addicted. Other great Philosophers such as Aristotle influenced him and Plato when he mentions that we cannot deny that man will always be drawn to what is considered unpardonable. Even "addicted" by the inconsistencies. This concept is also alluded to in many cultural stories reflected in Plato's writings on *Forms* as mentioned above in this text that describes Plato's writings on Truth, Beauty, and Goodness. *Rashomon*, the story mentioned earlier, attempts to convey how *Man* when he witnesses an unpardonable act is first disgusted, yet is often unaware of his own intentions to participate in the same level of behavior. We can conclude that it may be because *Man* is both good and bad and although *Man* is frequently disgusted by others' behavior has difficulty seeing this quality in themselves. Or, has difficulty accepting they too are capable of such unpardonable acts of true evil considered socially unacceptable.

Peirce mentions metaphysics; religion [God being real or not] as being a necessary component and has purposefulness because it is questioned, and makes a suggestion, and reference to how others may be led into believing in a God. Peirce is quoted as believing in a God. Yet, overall he contends there is no real basis to say it is so, or truth, but that the concept of believing has undeniable purposefulness. Removing the barriers to further inquiry holds significance.

In every culture, a belief in a being higher than oneself has importance to help humans make sense of the universe, and to feel a sense of connectedness; obtain meaning. Ultimately, believing in a God, or not, is a Saint Elmo's Fire effect in which hopefulness can be gained by adapting to a belief in the universe that will help appease people that the world is not overwhelmingly random and void of any certain meaning.

Charles Peirce also believed all *knowledge* can be provisional. When we investigate how the original 1952 *Diagnostic and Statistical Manual of Mental Disorders (DSM),* published by the American Psychiatric Association, attempts to classify Mental Disorders we began to see a pattern of how some Mental Illnesses are elaborated upon and extended over time, while some Mental Disorders become declassified, or deleted, and some remain provisional. For example, the concept and subsequent classification of the Mental Disorder of Schizophrenia has remained a provisional Disorder for over 100 years.

Emil Kraepelin, a German Psychiatrist, was the first to classify symptoms labeled *Dementia Praecox* in 1896. Kraepelin considered himself a scientific researcher first, and developed his construct of Dementia Praecox based on Esquirol's (1838) research efforts to differentiate hallucinations and illusions. Kraepelin also drew upon the work of Philippe Pinel's statistical research of classifying prisoners by age, disorder, and upon the work of Morel (1852) who is credited for coining the term *Demence Precoce* meaning a form of degenerative mental functioning leading to disability.

The symptoms Kraepelin researched and published would become the most widely accepted comprehensive classification to prove the beginning of the modern construct of Schizophrenia (Boyle, 1990). Even though Kraepelin's research studies were successfully documented as fact, his hypothesis statements and conclusions derived, were not necessarily truth, but continue to be considered provisional truths. Not factual conclusions drawn from his research but considered flawed interruptions extrapolated from the flawed data, as reported by Boyle many years later. Reportedly based on claims made by British researcher Boyle, Kraepelin conducted sloppy research studies making inferences from data he could not support as being fact then he went on to make subsequent statements of fact about what we find most commonly in those with Schizophrenia.

Scientific research studies are supposed to be conducted in very clear steps of progressive inferences based on facts you can prove. First, you make a hypothesis, make inferences, then test to see if those traits or symptoms can also be found and validated in larger study groups. Kraepelin did not take these scientific steps so widely accepted as standards of practice in conducting scientific research, and in concluding that Schizophrenia can be validated as something conclusive. The specific results Kraeplelin documented are considered vague, fragmented, and inconclusive. The diagnosis of Schizophrenia, although loosely supported in the research, gained a firm position in the literature, and remains provisional, which is suspect.

This provisional status of Schizophrenia remains true today partly due to the cluttered and complicated research documented in support of a diagnosis of Schizophrenia. The current research on Schizophrenia is so vast it spreads across multiple disciplines of Biology, Neurological research,

Family Systems Research, Genetic Research, and advanced Brain Mapping MRI technology. It becomes increasingly difficult for any one person to make sense of the findings. Moreover, then for those who attempt to make the research clear, our most brightest researchers in the field often end their research in favor of more lucrative fields of study. What remains is no concise documentation to argue if the diagnosis of Schizophrenia should be considered as no longer provisional, but downgraded to something less than what it is, or upgraded and its provisional status removed.

The question then becomes if Schizophrenia is a provisional Disorder, what should it be downgraded to, or what would need to occur in the field of research to conclusively finalize it into a more definitive Mental Health Disorder. To do so this author suspects, would leave a void for society to attach meaning to. After all it is clear patients who present with symptoms of Schizophrenia often require much needed antipsychotic medications to stabilize symptoms, also have a valid need for assistance for their ailments, have valid symptoms, and immediate need for extended social and financial supports.

Many controversial perspectives exist in this area of study which have eluded to the fact the reasons why persisting complications surrounding a provisional Clinical Diagnosis of Schizophrenia has been allowed to continue is partly due to our collective social constructs, and the potentiality for profits in treating those who have fallen under the construction of a Mental Health Care System.

By 1879, the first dedicated Psychological laboratory for research was established at the University of Leipzig, Germany, by Wilhelm Wundt to further our collective understanding of Psychology, marking the formal beginning of the study of human emotions, behaviors, and cognitions. He also proposed a paradigm for Experimental Psychology. Foundations for his work exhibited strong parallels to methods used in the science of Physics. It was not until 1883 the United States of America established its first Psychology laboratory at Johns Hopkins University. In 1890, New York State passed the State Care Act, ordering indigent Mentally Ill patients out of what were considered indigent care facilities, or poor *houses* and into Psychiatric State Hospitals for treatment. When the foundation was formed for the American Psychological Association (APA) in 1892 headed by G. Stanley Hall, it had a membership of 42. It would not be until 1953 the Association published a formal Code of Ethics for Psychologists.

Meanwhile significant publishing efforts were occurring to document scientific finding on the commercial uses for Psychological Diagnostic & Intelligence Testing (Alfred Binet, France, 1905), theories on Classical Conditioning by Ivan Pavlov (1906), the beginning of Behavioral Psychology as founded by John Watson (1913) & Behaviorism by B. F. Skinner (1953).

The field of Psychology also began to introduce by the 1900's a shift away from more scientific technical explanations biological brain dysfunctions to explain human nature and began to document scientific literature in support of a social component and personality influences to support the subtle nuances contributing to human nature.

Social Sciences

Psychology remains the youngest science in comparison to Physics or Biology. Gustav Fechner and Wilhelm Wundt have been credited with establishing Experimental Psychology in 1879.

The field of Social Sciences is concerned with the origins and development of human society to include the evolution of institutions, relationships, and ideas involved in social life. Psychology, Social Psychology, Sociology, Anthropology, Political Science, Economics, Law, and Criminology, are the disciplines dedicated to researching broad subject mater that affect societies belief systems most.

Western American thought perspectives concerning how to best study and describe society, has been influenced by ideas and insights gained from great Greek Philosophers Epicurus, Hippocrates, Plato, Aristotle, Italian Niccolò Machiavelli, originator of the idea of a political pragmatism that says the end justifies the means. Frenchman Jean Jacques Rousseau, and Englishmen Thomas Hobbes, John Locke, have contributed as well.

All sciences are now rooted in a code of Ethics to discover truth using a scientific method whereby scientific research experiments are conducted to objectively observe, describe, and to document accurately subjects or entities as they are without falsely introducing ones own personal preconceived world view, beliefs, or ideas. Furthermore, such claims derived from experiment results can then be judged as truth, new *knowledge,* or acceptable, based on the result's ability to be reproduced by another using the same methodology.

In many ways, the approach taken in the field of Physics is based on a Philosophy of conducting scientific research in a widely accepted systematic approach. Using a strictly constructed empirically proven method in science, researchers carefully develop a reasonable hypothesis they wish to either prove or disprove. Scientists are expected to use best practices in research, and then draw conclusions based on the results, which ultimately become the bases for new *knowledge* used to shape new beliefs regarding a given area of study. As in all well constructed research projects, research results based on scientific empirical research methods, are expected to be easily duplicated and their conclusions replicated by a third person to be considered substantial and true.

The core foundations of Modern Psychology, has a strong foundation in the Laws of Physics and in classical Athenian Philosophical Hypothesis Testing. Historically the Laws of Physics established itself as the basis of forming *knowledge,* but does not provide us with the *who* and *what* we are as human beings because not all human processes can be deduced to concepts measured in science. We can come close as has been speculated in Modern Psychology. The *who* and *what* we are as humans is well described in the literature, yet keep in mind there remains many Psychological Mental Health processes which remain provisional and evolving despite successes gained in the science of Psychology.

Physics and Quantum Physics contributed to the debate in furthering our understanding of human nature. After Socrates, Plato, Aristotle, Physicist began to argue why we exist, using the same arguments used some thousand years previously. Physicists also researched the elusive question are all things separate or interconnected. Physicists questioned why some things happen at a atomic level and some at a subatomic level. Does Science give us truth? In 1905, Albert Einstein established a idea of *Quanta* to explain the nature of light. Bohr would also work on Quantum Theory to help explain how atoms work. Einstein said God is subtle, but was not malicious. He would reveal the universe to us bit-by-bit, but not make it so hard we could not find the answers. Einstein felt Physics held the hidden secrets of the universe. Albert Einstein advanced physics as Charles Darwin did for biology. The debate continues however as to whether the study of people can or should be a science. So, in our intellectual debate to find the origins of human nature, we include theorists who talk about what is best overall for society. Are we as a society currently prepared for the next big Enlightenment in the field of Psychology? Can we predict the direction Psychology will go in the next century? Maybe what we can hope for in the future is a gradual unveiling of the Psychological processes that exist that prompts human beings to excel. Advanced research efforts are warranted to concentrate on motivational theory, virtues, and on what specific character traits increase the achievement of one's human potential. It is the hope we can explore more at our current boundaries, and discover something new.

From this point forward, even in our intellectual inquires across broad fields in scientific study; we find circular patterns of discussion, which reappear overtime. We came to understand evolution in a complex matrix. Evolution is apart of the explanation of how we came to be. Perhaps we as humans, at our core, are influenced more by our cognitive abilities. From this all mental processes of thought, feelings, senses or intuitive abilities, are derived. As a collective global society, we seek foremost to understand the universe, then to agree upon the most conducive manner in which humans should conduct their individual lives. Overtime we find there came punishment and confinement as a consequence for not leading a moral life, or for becoming a burden to society whether due to a lack of viable employment, inability to care for self, or being seen as sick or diseased by Mental Illness. Was there no room to include all in society, independent of levels of functioning? Acceptance of others in society or social ambivalence justified by a paradigm built upon social engineering?

The field of Modern Psychology is based on a firm foundation of Materialism. There remains however contradictory evidence regarding the Mentally Ill, yet perhaps it will take additional time to sort through the evidence or the development of a new theory yet to be constructed to instill in society the perception that greater insight is needed, the need to foster empowerment, and that it is compassionate to do so.

CHAPTER TWO

A Modern Psychological Approach

O n the road to becoming a Clinical Psychologist, the profession was full of
hope. Even today, many at increasingly higher rates continue to enroll
into our most prestigious universities to further the field of Psychological
Therapy techniques and the science of Psychology as a whole. On a more
broader level the field of Psychology was where the public turned for answers
on how to become fulfilled, to overcome common obstacles in daily living
and happiness, how to effectively resolve relationship conflicts, or to pursue
the elusive concept of achieving Self Actualization; Long Term Happiness.
Options available for those in society to achieve Psychological Growth beyond
the norm of only focusing clinical attention on those who are considered to
have the stigma of living with a Chronic Mental Health Illness, remains a
viable alternative for many.

The concept of an expanding Psychology was full of promise and was
expected to grow in its ability to be increasingly far more marketable than it
has ultimately become. In retrospect, throughout time, we have all relied on
the good nature and judgment found within us as individuals to navigate past
difficult situations. An understanding of how the Psychology of the human
mind works, helps us become less reactive and successful in overcoming life
dilemmas, yet with all the advances in the field to date, we find more of the

same and hopefuls offering *New Age Psychological Assumptions* which lead us to unsubstantial conclusions and disgruntled patrons. We deserve better.

We deserve a more comprehensive understanding of Psychology that can ultimately be applied to an empowering approach, one that fosters Psychological Growth in individuals.

What we seek is an experience. An experience to solidify new learning gained which will transform us from where we are currently in life. In all actuality, we as humans can only add to what is already there and strive to identify that part of us which is never changing from its fundamental core roots. To change ones fundamental roots is not possible no matter how aggressively a new Psychological concept is marketed to the mass media for the fundamental goal of financial product profit. We can however, in Psychology add to what is already there, or as individuals shift the manner in which we go about day-to-day interactions to make them more productive interactions, both in our understanding of the world and behaviors that will lead to new positive actions taken.

Perhaps what we do best in our collective role as Psychologists is to allow individuals increasingly demanding incremental opportunities to expand the depth of their current view of self, and their unique view of current life situations they may encounter at various developmental stages of life. Consequently allowing for the expanding of their lens through which they view the world that filters all they encounter into something more inline with that which the patient desires to become. There will always be a necessary component of patient's *Taking Action* and remains today a less emphasized component to Professional Therapy in our current traditional Psychological approaches executed in the practice of Modern Day Clinical Psychology Practices.

We are not faulty at our core. We are not defective, but built for greatness and some arrive at their full potential at different stages of development. The first personal mandate should not be that "*I must change*," but rather to question "*how can I become more?*" This empowering perspective allows us to nourish that part of us that is good and worthy. In essence, we add to what already exists. This is the first shift in perspective that will naturally foster more. Becoming fulfilled individually, healthy, balanced, achieving increased Psychological Normalcy comes from a healthy foundation and sustained efforts to nurture what already exists. As in nature new growth forms from the continued nurturing, not the continued neglect and breaking down of the established core roots.

The Helping Profession

These following chapters will explore the value of what a basic understanding of how the field of Psychology has evolved overtime from the author's unique vantage point as a Clinical Psychologist. The reader may find comfort in learning that not all life dilemmas we find in life are symptomatic, abnormal, but apart of developing.

Psychologists, Psychiatrists, Medical & Health Care Professionals, Couples Therapist, Sex Therapists, Employee Assistance Program Specialists, and the broader helping professions, will discover distinctive nuances of empowerment crucial today for understanding, facilitating, and affecting change within those we seek to help.

It is difficult not to be a bit basis to the field of Professional Clinical Psychology as a Psychologist. The field of Psychology is considered the most inclusive of all disciplines under the broad umbrella of Mental Health Services. Practicing within the field of Psychology is the author's profession of choice, and have years of experience to validate it as the most rewarding career choice. Over the years in periods where I have often questioned my choice of profession, all the self-appointed mentors I learned from along the way in postgraduate studies who so graciously encouraged eager students in class to ponder a while on why they entered a helping profession as a career always reminded me.

New Psychologists may be asked by professors to question why they entered the field for many reasons. One reason professors ask is to question students' motivation and commitment to the field. The other reason is to analyze unrealistic expectations a student may have in *helping* others, or to address any student delusional ill conceived notions they may have in their ability to cure the world, or to confront the student's need to satisfy their own self reflected *sense of self* needs often referred to as *The Wounded Healer* effect. Other reasons professors may entertain this line of questioning in class is to allow students to ponder the realities of the profession. To ponder further the inevitable harsh realities all Psychologists may face at one point in their career. In doing so may prepare new Psychologists how to respond to such realities as they may surface. The field of Professional Psychology as a profession has a way of affecting people in inconceivable ways unknown to the inexperienced clinician. Compassionate Fatigue can manifest after years of practicing in the field with difficult patients, or the Psychologist may over the years begin questioning whether they are really making *meaningful impact* with their patients. These expected predicaments can all take its toll overtime on the professional with unrealistic expectations of the profession as a whole. Professors asking students to ponder *"why am I doing this?"* It is a question for reflection of one's intentions for entering the field of Psychology.

In my experience those in class who were ask to ponder this important question were either passionate about what they wanted to do with Psychology, while others were returning students and had already witnessed first hand the value in providing services to people and knew the real value in *helping*. It is in the doing Psychological treatment one can experience the benefits others receive from it first hand. The result of what patients actually receive is unique and different every time based on their Psychologist and interpretation of their individual experience with the process.

In a class asked this question, as a returning student who had already worked in the field as a Psychological Therapist with a Masters of Science in Counseling Psychology (MS) degree for several years prior to returning to school to complete a Doctoral Program degree of Clinical Psychology, the realities of the profession were already known. The benefits of working as a Therapist, the benefits of therapy, and experience gained from years working as a facilitator on numerous Psychological Growth Retreats with clients allowed for realistic clarity of what the profession had to offer others. I believed I was in good company along with other returning students in my class who also possessed practical experience in witnessing first hand what changing transformations can occur under the right circumstances through an *active* therapy process. I continue to believe changes that can occur for clients in a *active* therapy process is nothing short of amazing. Especially when noticeable successes were gained by clients during the process. Anyone who has experienced a transformation can attest what I speak of. It is internal. Others can see it. It is a true phenomenon that occurs at a deep and personal level that can impact ones psyche to the point it can change ones perspective, creates a change in ones world values, ultimately affecting character, drive, and internal motivation levels to pursue more in life.

This is the stuff of nirvana in some respects many speak of. If you look up nirvana its fantasy, illusion, and if it takes hold long enough to affect lasting shifts in a individual's world perspective, then the reality is to the beholder. This is not fantasy. What we strive for becomes reality as well as what we individually focus on. There are no mistakes and nirvana is a state from which most take great notice of, question, and then begin to take action towards addressing individual life dilemmas.

What I do know is individuals who undergo a compassionate form of Psychological Therapy can experience pleasure in finding focus and meaning for ones own life. From this renewed focus individuals initiate new behaviors and actions to make their goals a reality. What we as *Professionals* choose to call the affect is only secondary to the impact achieved by most willing to allow another to facilitate the process and opportunity.

How Can I Help

The second fundamental philosophy I have come to adopt over the years from my experience starting out as a Psychological Therapist that later translated into professional success gained as I practiced as a Clinical Psychologist in a Psychiatric Hospital setting was to always approach a new patient with my own internal questioning of *"how can I help?"* first, and foremost. Next, the professionals calculated intent to execute a sustained focus of fostering a patient's inner strengths to process the truth underlying their *crisis* has proven overtime to be effective in efforts to facilitate treatment plan interventions with patients in personal crisis.

A targeted focus of increasing an individual's sense of empowerment where clients can begin to widen by substantial degrees their individual vision of where their true strengths and abilities lie. Additionally, patients I have noticed often require subtle reminding that they are the best ones to advocate for themselves to gain mastery over their own sense of self-empowerment skills and resourcefulness. We often underestimate another's ability to access their individual dilemmas. We assume because they have ask for help, they are just plum out of options for themselves. On the contrary, I have learned over the years working with patients admitted against their will into a Psychiatric Hospital many have the capacity to process their dilemmas effectively. While patients are in a state of personal crisis, and help was provided them by a forced legal process to protect either themselves or others in society, the trained professional quickly discovers these patients also possess great insight if allowed the space and time to process past their immense internal crisis they were enduring. A professional's ability to foster insight in ones patient is only half the dilemma, the true work is in fostering the patient to see the need to execute new skills or actions based on new insights.

When a patient is ask, *"how can I help?"* What is it you need most now? Or, *"tell me more about what led up to your hospitalization?"* The dynamics of the situation seemingly changes between the patient and Psychologist relationship. The mind requires time to process and make sense of the entirety of the situation before feeling they can go forward to resolve dilemmas. It is a slow painstakingly unique individual internal process many must choose for themselves. The Psychologist who carefully allows for the safe space for patients to process the full magnitude of their seemly overwhelming situation, are more successful with patients over time.

As a Psychologist, to facilitate improvement in patients I practice a core belief we must consider the whole person and all of a patient's life experiences they bring into the therapy process to foster internal motivation levels. Patients encountered in a Psychiatric Hospital setting who when ask about what they feel they need to overcome a current crisis or life dilemma creating undue conflicts, knew exactly what it was they should do, or knew what would be required of them to regain balance and stability in their lives, but voiced little motivation to do so.

Often what was required was new learning to see them past obstacles they had no expertise in previously. When patients entered into a new hospitalization, which was just the précipice of previous faulty decision-making, or lengthy periods of substance abuse, many ask for answers. Or, displayed a willingness to participate in opportunities to gain new strategies they could implement to create a compelling future for themselves. Most Psychiatric Hospitals require it mandatory for inpatients to participate in group activities prior to discharge and if they do not, ones discharge can be delayed conveniently at the discretion of the admitting facility. Nonetheless, once a patient becomes a active group member, their participation will mandate a certain level of willingness on the patient's behalf often manifesting itself through a slow process of one feeling a sense of cohesiveness based on shared experiences the Psychologist can create among its group members.

Becoming a danger to oneself or other people, is the defining line that separates a human's ability to make good decisions for themselves, and may require a forced hospitalization to regain stability.

Most do not remain in this state of personal crisis, as it is humanly difficult to sustain. The crisis fades with time and those who can sustain this state of personal Psychological upheaval overtime are considered to have deeper neurological disturbances that may be assessed to warrant repeated involuntary Psychiatric hospitalizations and psychotropic medications to treat presenting symptoms and stabilize the patient over time. This latter category has a valid fundamental scientific biological basis for receiving a concrete American Psychiatric Association Diagnostic Disorder as well as other peripheral chronic Life Management symptoms prompting states of repeated forced Psychiatric Hospitalizations have been attributed to nuances uniquely associated to North American medical practices.

Legally forced Psychiatric Hospitalizations, commonly referred to as a 5150 Order, have a clear criteria and the truly Chronically Mentally Ill Psychotic patient, or patients considered to possess Chronically Mentally Ill recurrent Depressive Mood states with self harm tendencies, harm to others, or considered gravely disabled, in the research are found in far less numbers compared to those populations in other developing nations in comparison to North America. The growing demand for additional Mental Health Psychiatric Care Services in North America has risen since 1950. If researched carefully the astute and curious intellectual will find evidence for this modern day occurrence commonly referred to as a alarming phenomena to have contributing factors linked to society's political decisions to fund social programs, or not. Decisions our society embraces as rule regarding the funding of social programs are often formulated from the larger collective social norms of the day based on what society would agree on as being normal behavior, and what small population in society is considered in need of greater financial assistance, access to resources, from the whole of society. Creative social engineering of values and random judgments we so commonly make as a society about those who exist in our society with behavioral characteristics deemed by the society as inappropriate, or those unwilling to care for themselves, are also contributing factors which continue to dictate overriding political policies.

We as a North American society are left ultimately to allow others in policy making positions to determine for the general masses what an appropriate level of behavioral acceptability is. Because of the collective moral judgments we make, most in society are comfortable allowing elected officials to absorb the burden of determining and making decisions that impact the collective whole of society. Ultimately, those policies made dictate the care of those who cannot care for themselves. It is a great burden. Surprisingly enough since the 1950's, it remains inconclusive if rather those in need of increased social financial support dictate political policy contributing to the increasing numbers of patients with repeated Mental Health Psychiatric crises, or whether more Psychological guidance and Psychological education is needed for this masses in the North American population to curb the rise in forced Psychiatric Hospitalizations. Access to services is limited, therefore; savvy consumers must gain access by adapting and being the most in need. Therein lies the vicious cycle we all contribute to.

Many patients however I encountered within a Psychiatric Hospital setting would inevitability express a sense of hope during their admission that their life would turn around and this alone would allow patients to give themselves permission to attend group after group in the hospital until discharge. My patients, who showed the greatest recovery rates after their initial crisis stage, took a vested interest in exploring information geared towards alternatives they could incorporate into new behaviors, increase one's personal responsibilities after discharge, and could verbalize an initial plan. Identifying support systems, medications management, and expressing increased willingness to motivate themselves should another personal crisis surface, showed the greatest promise for recovery at discharge.

One motivation for publishing this text was another observation I made while in a Psychiatric Hospital setting and that was the discharge interview with the identified patient, and their immediate family members, or spouse. I found it alarming at how many Family Therapy sessions or Couples Therapy sessions I facilitated prior to discharge where a family system or marriage dynamics often played center stage in fueling the crisis modes in patients. I would spend time with patients in group learning about their unique life dynamics, and presenting Mental Health symptoms, only to find at the discharge interview with supportive family members that the family system dynamics was also an issue in need of further sessions to ensure the identified patient's personal crisis would not resurface. Not only was I able to identify a progressive negative pattern over time in Family Therapy Sessions, but wanted to explore more personally what faulty dynamics were at play and the obstacles most patients found difficult to address when discharged into the rigors of daily living with family members.

Modern Perceptions Of Mental Illness

According to Goffman (1961) the career of the Chronic Mental Health patient can be divided into three distinct phases. The first is the phase before hospitalization. Second, is the phase in the hospital, and third, is the phase after discharge from the Psychiatric Hospital setting while out in the community. The focus for the patient is on the social *self* as it adjusts to an environment where the individual can be then judged as sick, even though the patient may not consider themselves as ill despite recurrent negative consequences from their behaviors, feedback they receive from society, the chaos generated, or feedback received from their family involvements. It can be equated to a long series of denial. The personal experiences felt as a direct result of undergoing an initial hospitalization for acute psychotic symptoms often compared to similar experiences of those undergoing a form of trauma. The assigned diagnosis by the attending Psychiatrist, or Psychologist, can be met by the *designated patient* with resistance and shock by most patients. The immediate reaction to not identify with *having a Mental Health Disorder* is extremely common and often repeated in the literature as a contributor leading to repeated relapses among those deemed to have Chronic Mental Illness.

While experiencing the trauma of obtaining a new Clinical Mental Health Disorder, one which traditionally carries a high price of social stigma attached, the reality becomes clearer at this point to most patients a reduced lifestyle may have to be undergone while attending to the early interventions necessary to effectively manage and stabilize ones new diagnosis. Regardless if the diagnosis given is a chronic form of Schizophrenia, or some form of Depressive Mood Disorder, the adjustment to such a label can be traumatic for most. Often lethargic moods are common in acute patients hospitalized as they adjust to a new Clinical Diagnosis. The depths of despair, and feelings of hopelessness, and helplessness become their reality accordingly making a choice to become excited about the possibility of recovery may be premature. Yet, the importance of engaging in repeated discussions with patients to consider future symptom improvement is paramount.

The establishment of a clear and calculated approach to discharge treatment planning with patients undergoing such a adjustment will stand a better prognosis if treatment plans can incorporate educational sessions to inform patients of their chance for future symptom improvement, mandatory discussions regarding side effects with psychotropic medications prescribed, and discussion on the benefits of receiving future Psychological treatment after discharge including Family Therapy Sessions, are all strongly recommended to stabilize patients.

If patients become informed about success rates for their assigned Mental Health inflection, now commonly found with Schizophrenia populations, the chances of recovery increase according to Kruger, (2000). Kruger explains that just by the addition of *hope* if it is communicated to people that their chances for recovery are roughly estimated to be very good at 65%, 50% as a more conservative figure, patients may become less content to simply exist in a state of inactivity. Consequently, when they experience symptoms of hallucinations or delusions, they may find the strength to persist through the pain of symptoms knowing they will end. Research more widely distributed to the masses on recovery rates sets an expectation for patients and the research shows that when Mental Health consumers are informed about what to expect overtime with specific Clinical Mental Health Diagnoses, significant improvement surprisingly occurs.

There is research into the correlates between hopefulness and cerebral functions that show hope engages the involvement of brain areas that deal with the functions of cognition, language, perception, vision, audition, and emotions according to Gottschalk, France, & Buchsbaum, (1993). Therefore, we can conclude that with the introduction of hope, specific areas of the brain activate affecting one's ability to engage with self and others. Patient motivation levels can increase through the fostering of hope with the simple routine of Psychologist and Psychiatrists making it a priority to always ensure they incorporate into patient treatment plans a Psychological Educational component to provide information about the Diagnosis assigned and recovery rates to be expected over time.

Motivation can drive patients to become active members on their individual treatment teams, contributing on the team, instead of becoming outsiders of their primary treatment structure that dictates their level of care. Moreover, influencing the patient's chance to improve their quality of life. If patients know they will recover, and are expected to improve overtime, patients also become more aware that they have a positive future ahead of them to build on. Hence, placing the patient in a vantage point to create their own compelling future one which has positive affects on mood, internal motivation levels and stands to decrease Depressive states of hopelessness and recurrent lethargic inactivity.

Increased Hope and Taking Action

Hope is the enemy of change if not combined with taking progressive action. This is a rather profound statement since in our society we are convinced through years of exposure to popular culture, to believe in concepts of "having faith" and that all matters difficult, will be magically transformed into something more rewarding if we only *believe*, hope, and seek the support of others who are also faithful. As a Psychologist I am convinced that this perception is although useful, can be most damaging. One, if we believe all will be okay it provides the rationalization in most to not do what is necessary by all means to ensure matters really do resolve in the manner they would like. To be effective and fulfilled we must foster and nurture the future.

Change occurs through the continuous and often sobering understanding that something must be accepted and changed.

Perception is everything. Our discernment or insight on a dilemma is as important as discussing the situation. It is a mindset of believing you can conquer personal obstacles verses a *can't* mentality. When someone seeks my services and responds, "I can't" to a concern that has begun to interfere with well being I never respond with "Why not?" This would be judgmental. I have come to know that often people may have good reasons as to why they *can't* and I see it as my job to understand their beliefs and perceptions surrounding this issue or problem at hand they have not been able to resolve on their own.

Most do not decide to win in advance. This is neither wrong or right, but when a patient begins to be affected significantly by a negative life situation because of their lack of internal motivation to address it, then and only then is it problematic. From here, we can address the conflict between what a patient is saying and what they are doing. To muster up inner strength to follow through takes drive. It takes strength of character, more precisely internal courage to address the discontinuity expressed and commitment to *taking action* to limit ones personal discomfort felt. To be reminded of what one values can have immense benefits.

When we place value on something, we find a way to make it happen no matter the cost. The human fascination we have with overcoming odds is translatable to all. Take the Special Olympics. Most enjoy viewing the struggle and astonishing accomplishments leading to success over defeat. Defeating all odds to persevere. The viewer of such a Special Olympics event wants to push then along if they could, and if the viewer physically could, those in the game would say "Don't you dare!" We all need to experience the joy of defeating that which is a challenge. You see it is in the personal experience of victory felt, we gain individual confidence in our ability to conquer the next problem and personal challenges.

Similarly, in treatment Psychologists should not want their patients to be cheated out of an experience to initiate and create experiences they can conquer and feel victorious over. Many in the professional field of documenting the *process of therapy* would term this effect as pacing and leading. If the *process* is executed properly its effect can lead to new patient learning on how to initiate for themselves how to take steps towards achieving incremental successes well past your involvement with them.

Patients learn far more personally about their individual ability to motivate themselves from the trail and error of initiating and overcoming difficulty with increased support, then by the Psychologist aggressively taking the lead with their patients. Psychologists may assume the role of leading their patient's by the hand every step of the way in the Therapy process and may inadvertently limit a patient's ability to learn how to master internal steps necessary to feel empowered in the future when other obstacles present themselves. The *process of therapy* is also considered a process of instilling patient empowerment if applied ethically. Additionally a well-known taboo in the field of Mental Health Managed Care is to keep patients in treatment far longer than is effective, which is equally counter productive for the patient. This practice of care can be viewed as a way for Mental Health providers to accrue additional financial security over time, but does little good for the patient who desires to get well and to then move on outside of a treatment setting and live a more fulfilling lifestyle.

Patients must adapt the mind set failing is not an option when pursuing goals to resolve a difficult life dilemma. Non judgmentally we confront patients to motivate themselves towards wanting victory over their problematic situation. The nuances at play within a therapy process is vulnerable to many factors and effective therapy incorporates a plan to instill components of self-empowerment into the therapy process. When a person does not know what to do, or have a good handle on what steps are necessary to significantly impact goals which will lead to obtainment, passion alone can provide the fuel for individuals. With each success made, momentum gained can spark the interest of others to give a helping hand and place them in a better position to obtain more knowledge so they can go on to sustain more success' over time. Action leads to momentum and allows for greater proximity to ones ultimate destination, not sitting on the sidelines contemplating how nice it would be to achieve all they desire.

From a philosophical perspective, the difference between sanity and insanity would be a matter of exacting balance. According to Krishnamurti, (1996), sanity is to be whole, non-fragmented in action, in life, in every kind of relationship, which is the very essence of sanity. Sanity means to be whole, and healthy. To be insane, neurotic, psychotic, unbalanced, Schizophrenic, whatever name you might give to it, is to be fragmented, broken up in action and in movement of relationship, which is existence.

Philosophers discuss the truth of existence and how painful it can be. To exist with the unpleasantness of life, the realities of everyday life, mixed with both good and bad. As humans, we seek honestly something secure and consistently pleasant always mindful to limit pain when possible, and the avoidance of the self. A common fundamental problem that faces every individual is the experience of psychological pain that corrodes all thinking and feeling.

A popular question many Philosophers have pondered is if it is possible to teach another how to end pain. If a person can be taught how to end pain, would pain cease?

I question in keeping with this topic of Mental Health and expectations of patients, if patients could be taught how to remit Mental Health symptoms, would their pain and suffering cease? Philosophers would concede that a person can learn a technique for ending pain, be it physical or Psychological pain, but in the very process of ending one particular pain, a new type of pain comes into being. In the process of overcoming trauma, one finds trust in self and others. New relationships formed become more pleasurable with increased trust for others. The process of overcoming the pain of coping with a Mental Health Illness, one discovers the challenges of daily living rewarding, yet new challenges surface. And, with this comes new sources of stress and Depression to address as they discover that being themselves is not normal or acceptable in the society and they must adapt and conform to someone else's standard of *Psychological Normalcy*. Adapting then becomes the new source of Psychological pain felt.

All individuality is lost in the process of conforming, and is a form of new pain on a personal level. Meaning, the experience of discovering you are a failure at adjusting to current social norms of morality, or behavior, is at the core of not being accepted by the larger whole of society.

Michel Foucault, French Philosopher and intellectual, wrote a series of text most famous for *Madness and Civilization, The Birth of the Clinic, The Order of Things, Discipline and Punish,* and *The History of Sexuality.* Within his series *Madness and Civilization,* Foucault explained that in taking the "mad" out of confinement during the 18th century asylums, patients then became subject to new levels of fearsome tests as they strove to conform to society's standards of morality and normal behavior. A similar incidence still exists in the form of patient outcomes and societies expectations from the Mentally Ill (Fillingham, 1993).

In the construction of Mental Health treatment plans for the Mentally Ill, words like appropriate treatment interventions, increase social skills, decrease cognitive distortions, and learn more adaptive coping skills to manage illness, are commonly prescribed by Psychologist, Therapists, and Case Managers on treatment teams. We also find with more Chronic Mental Health patients the need to heavily medicate patients to counter Psychosis or Depressive Moods and increase hopefulness if patients have resorted to suicidal behaviors to relieve their pain and suffering.

The truth of the matter, in a purely philosophical global perspective, *hope* is the enemy of change. Without the fuel of *taking action* to propel necessary changes to one's life in daily living, everything remains the same. The component of *taking action* and displaying behavioral changes must be combined with *hope* if a change in symptoms is to occur. To foster *hope* is important. Without *hope*, motivation levels dwindle because there becomes nothing to strive for, no compelling future can be foreseen by the patient, and often *hope* provides the motivation to work towards an end goal. One must first trust in the possibility that some greater good will result if they do the necessary work first. Patients succumbing to vague treatment team plans (e.g., increase social skills) may be only addressing surface concerns and bypassing an opportunity to influence ones core symptoms by understanding what they must do as "patient."

This author feels what is happening now in the field of Psychology is a shifting in our social consciousness as many work to create the environment to get others heading in the right direction toward symptom improvement and recovery. The concept of *hope* in the most simplest of terms, is an illusion.

Perhaps not truth, but mental defaults our minds resort to for escape from fear or pain. Krishnamurti (1996) acknowledged the reason why *hope* is so indispensable to life for humans is that if we understood the problem there would be no need for hope. He explained if you observe your own mind, you will see that when you are in discomfort, in conflict, in misery, your mind seeks a way away from it. The process of going away from the problem is the creation of *hope*.

Therefore, the mind going away from the problem creates fear; the very movement of going away, the flight from the problem is fear and *hope* is necessary for comforting the mind in the mist of fear. *Hope* then provides the comfort and the motivation to forge onward in life. What then becomes important is how the mind regards the problem. Even in despair, with *hope*, problems become more manageable, and the ability to understand the unconceivable is possible transforming a once painful existence into one more manageable.

Effective Mental Health Treatment Plans with patients therefore must combine a equal amount of attention to individual patient motivation levels to gain stability, a Psychological Education component and strategies focused on overcoming the patient's unique life obstacles, and compassionate confrontation to increase individual motivation levels. This is the challenge to all Mental Health providers and seemingly the most complex for most professionals to implement, yet remains the crust of the core work for most Psychologist and Psychiatrists who work with patients.

The Allure Of Working With The Chronically Mentally Ill

Working with the chronically Mentally Ill is a challenge and an exceptional training opportunity for new Psychologists and Psychiatrists. The population offers a wide variety of symptoms often presented within The American Psychiatric Association *Diagnostic and Statistical Manual of Mental Disorders* Fourth Edition Text Revision (DSM- IV-TR) (2000). On average, we find either professionals in the field who are new to the profession and seek intensive training with exposure to a chronic population, or are ambitious talented professionals who work in this area, and whom then move on to other populations. For those who stay, their prospects of financial gain rest in publishing their experiences and research findings about the population. Much of the research funding by large Mental Health Agencies, including State and Federal sources, have improved treatment outcomes and subsequent long term care, but sadly most have closed completely or have shifted their focus to more profitable areas of managed care.

State Psychiatric Hospitals have experienced substantial downsizing or wide closures of hospitals that traditionally provided primary care for the severe and chronically Mentally Ill populations. Due to limited funding to treat this population, often our brightest, and most ambitious Psychologists, Psychiatrists, and Clinical Researchers, with the most experience in the field, move on to other more career satisfying populations. As a result, fewer professionals remain to carefully examine inconsistencies that heavily blanket this segment of Psychology.

Our current information concerning longitudinal research with Schizophrenic populations detailing expectations for symptom improvement overtime has been here all along, distribution to a wider audience of professionals and consumers however has been limited. The literature is too complicated and overwhelming to weed through to make sense of the material, and there exists a controversial side of medicating Schizophrenic patients. Presently, large pharmaceutical organizations are vested in influencing the direction of the American Psychiatric Association that can create dual relationships and an unfair basis towards prescribing one psychotropic medication over the other. No mistaking psychotropic medications delivery is a big business and can be quite influential to the industry as a whole.

The concept of Mental Illness, and its treatment, in part, is built and sustained on a social construct, which few are willing to challenge. If the current social construct were challenged successfully, a deconstructionist theory would not allow for a proper replacement to adequately address the existing concern.

For the reasons that there is an ingrained mind set that it is inhumane not to treat those who cannot provide for themselves, but immersed in the care of those who cannot help themselves, becomes burdensome to society. Despite the inconsistencies between what a society wishes to do and its ability to acknowledge its limitations, what results is a system that has taken on a powerful life of its own.

In our society's efforts to treat the mentally insane, an imbalance has occurred wherein chronic Mentally Ill populations still require assistance no matter what the American public chooses to label the affliction. The pharmaceutical companies profit. Financial funding annually is spent to address all forms of Mental illness' and there is a trickle down affect; Psychiatrists are gainfully employed who prescribe medications, those who conduct research and development for new and exciting promising medications secure continued employment, and Psychologists benefit from treating patient's symptoms. There is also substantial employment in researching the core cause of major Psychotic Disorders such as Schizophrenia, and the like, to which many disciplines compete against one another for notable recognition in their field of choice. Make no mistake, the business of perpetuating "illness" is big business and where you find prospects to make new profits, American diligence has proven over the centuries, the industrious are swift and cleaver in adapting and manipulating social constructs.

Consumers of Mental Health or those in need of social assistance due to poverty will always in increasing numbers become savvy as well in adapting to a social system that rewards social conformity.

In Practice

Where we are with Modern Day Clinical Psychology Practices is the continued focus on illness and what is wrong. Those with substantial chronic Mental Illness makes up only a small percentage of all Mental Illness' Diagnosed through out Northern America and the world, yet yields the greatest amount of financial burden to our global expenditures for treatment. A subsequent peripheral effect of this type of focus is it only renders more consumerism in the form of Psychology Courses to learn about the history of Psychology. More State Universities to teach us about Psychologies long past, Mental Health providers who aggressively conduct market analysis of communities before setting up shop to ensure they can achieve a return on investment for their services offered. There is little to do anymore with focused research, which will educate the public how to increase ones level of resilience, self-sufficiency, and to feel fulfilled in their day-to-day living. Allowing for more balance in our research efforts would render remarkable impact in societies understanding of fundamental beliefs of how we all can manage life more effectively past the dilemmas we all endure.

This is not to say at different stages of development we all encounter some form of Mental Illness, but rather if a global consciousness exists that only focuses on Illness, it can erroneously perpetuate the neediness in those who by default of not having other viable options for thriving, resort to fitting into what exists to satisfy one's needs. When expectations are set at a higher level of functioning, even with a Mental Illness, behavior and perceptions change to fit into what is expected of those in society. Social norms are always perpetuated by what is accepted by society and rewarded.

What do twenty-first century Psychology Strategists offer? Positive Psychology, a relatively new approach to Psychology founded by Psychologist, Dr. Martin Seligman, contends that happiness may have a baseline and when unforeseen circumstances occur he explains for example winning the lottery, or becoming paralyzed, appear to have only slight impact on one's level of sustained perceived quality of happiness over time. In a systematic study of 22 people who won major lotteries Dr. Seligman found that patients reverted to their baseline level of happiness over time, winding up no happier than 22 matched controls (Seligman, 2002).

Current research on happiness results in a disparity of results available compared to the amount of research available on Chronic Mental Illness. According to Psychologist, Dr. Tal Ben-Shahar, Harvard Professor, who received recognition for offering a course at the prestige Harvard University campus titled *The Science of Happiness* was referred to in media coverage as unprecedented. So much so it gained the attention of CBS News who conducted an Interview with the Professor to learn more about the effects his students gained from completing his course on happiness. According to the professor, Positive Psychology puts a smile on everybody's face by teaching students about happiness. Dr. Ben-Shahar's course is reported as a new class at Harvard University which puts classes like Calculus and Russian Literature to the side for something more unusual. The course focuses on the Psychological aspects of a fulfilling and flourishing life to include topics of happiness, self-esteem, empathy, friendship, love, achievement, creativity, music, spirituality, and humor.

In Dr. Ben-Shahar's course he allows the class to contemplate what meaning we can gain from where as a field Psychology places its greatest efforts and resources. In a review of research based on Psychological Abstracts from 1997-2000, he concluded that there was a ratio of 21 to 1 in favor of research which focused on negative symptoms of Mental Illness compared to qualities that are believed to enhance our lives as people.

Emotional States & Number of Research Studies Conducted 1997 - 2000

Anger:	5,584	Joy:	415
Anxiety:	41,416	Happiness:	1,710
Depression:	54,040	Life Satisfaction:	2,582

Ratio: 21/1

Table: 1 Mental Health Abstracts Research Results 1997-2000 by Emotional States Published by Psychologist, Dr. Tal Ben-Shahar.

Because Dr. Ben-Shahar's course was viewed as unprecedented in the field of Professional Psychology and immensely beneficial for the students who gave such rave reviews, a line of questioning surfaced as to why there are not more opportunities for such a course available in all universities as a standard. Some variation in its basic intent available to all due to our collective societal basic value system to promote all subject matter which is life enhancing. It is suspected what plays a large role in more professionals in the field not focusing research efforts on this type of information is the individual perception of how much control they have over the field and comfort with going with the status quo. That which should be done is not always executed for a number of reasons in part due to financial funding obstacles we face as a Professional Psychological Profession and product of sorts this author concluded.

Are individuals in North American society able to decipher our current knowledge in Psychology and translate this into every day life to improve their lives? Is there more we need to make clear in the field of Psychology? Does society need clarification, or are we as consumers of Psychological products driven only by current research; content with the status quo? Are we content with the level of current accessibility to information and strategies?

Some would argue people in general do not want the answers to fulfillment, what they seek is a safe harbor void of choices and responsibility. The danger in this is it breeds states of helplessness and hopelessness, and ultimately Depressive Mood states of resignation in Mental Health consumers, and for professionals in the field of Mental Health decreased motivation to research those topics that would have greater impact on society. Individual perceptions of how much control they have to either initiate beneficial projects, or follow the status quo regardless of competing social or value conflicts, have a direct correlation to ones feeling of powerlessness and social learning theories of internal and external control (Phares, 1976; Rotter, 1966). Concepts of personal courage to be explored more in later chapters, is what fuels one's desire to initiate novel projects seen as beneficial, despite anticipated rewards.

As reported in the American Psychological Association (APA) *Monitor Magazine*, following its 2006 Annual Convention in New Orleans, the popular television personality, Dr. Phil McGraw, Ph.D., received a feature article in the magazine for his contribution as a keynote speaker at the APA convention held that year.

Television personality, Dr. Phil McGraw, aims to make concepts and strategies found within Psychology accessible to the general public they might not otherwise understand. Through his show and life strategy books he has authored on topics ranging from general Psychological issues of parenting, weight loss, or abusive relationships, Dr. McGraw has gained popularity in national television ratings with his commitment to communicate that *life can be different* and professionals can help people to thrive. Dr. McGraw states his show provides a starting point for professional help, and his show should never be construed as a substitute for traditional Psychological Therapeutic services. All the while, his training is that matched with the most established of Psychologist who practice under the ethical codes of a professional license and knowledge base. Contents of any typical Dr. Phil Show is evaluated to provide the audience thought provoking psychological strategies and insights that contain a level of Psychological sophistication and training in analyzing human relationships.

The Argument In Support Of A Shifting Consciousness

So what do we need? Some novel format to present Psychological information, but with a thin veil of magical entertaining illusion that mysteriously removes all social stigma made possible by a carefully crafted disclaimer so the consumer will not believe the process they are undergoing is Psychological Therapy. To make the benefits of Psychology more accessible to all we may require a shift in societal perception about the benefits of Psychology, one that fosters more education, a focus on personal strengths, a focus on concepts of empowerment, character over virtue, and a simplicity towards compassion, over ego.

The irony is that if Dr. McGraw was not subject to ethical recourse with the American Psychological Association (APA), he would be perhaps practicing Psychology in a different format void of the need to add a disclaimer to the services he offers millions through his popular mass media television broadcasts.

His knowledge base for Psychology is that of any licensed regulated clinician so what he offers on television is a glimpse into sound Psychological Strategies viewers can learn from and translate into their daily lives, some receiving lasting benefit from the new education. The one component his popular television show lacks is the ability to monitor the effects his information has on viewers hence therein lies the liability and subsequent need for a disclaimer that his services should never be a substitute for Professional Psychological Therapeutic Services. Personal advancements are always possible regardless of the venue when people are allowed the space and time to observe their situation honestly, reach threshold, and take decisive action accordingly.

Benefits of Psychotherapy

Individual change occurs by taking more responsibility over what the individual wishes to achieve. Therapy is mentoring, providing opportunities to learn new skills, and maneuvering the patient with great finesse towards a direction more in line with what the patient has voiced they desire to attain. Take any approach and you will receive the same results. Psychological Therapy also referred to as Psychotherapy is an important form of treatment for a host of psychological problems, including low self-esteem, social problems, anxiety disorders, sadness, thought disturbances, and substance abuse. But, is Psychotherapy effective? For years, Clinical Psychologists have debated the assumed benefits of Psychotherapy. Many studies have compared Psychotherapy to various drug treatments to no treatment at all. By statistically combining hundreds of these studies, researchers have confirmed that overall, Psychotherapy is better than no treatment at all. These studies have shown that most patients who improve with Psychotherapy do so within six months of beginning treatment.

Surprisingly, these studies also indicate all major types of Psychotherapy, despite differences in theoretical orientations, or in techniques used, are about equally effective. Psychologists theorize that despite surface differences, all Psychotherapies have in common three factors that help to promote change in patients. The necessary components are that they have one, a supportive and trusting relationship with the therapist. Two, patients are allowed an opportunity to open up and talk freely. Lastly, the patient should possess a positive expectation for improvement.

Clinical Psychiatric interventions using psychotropic medications compared to Psychotherapy alone each have their own benefits. When both are used together remains the industry standard for the best clinical outcomes. The optimal treatment course recommended should include both a Psychotherapy component and Psychiatric interventions as warranted.

Self-motivational self-help dogma also has merit yet their sole use should _only_ be recommended depending on the severity of the issue targeted, and level of impact this issue has on one's Psychological Social Functioning. Therefore, counseling approaches devoted to healing modern day-to-day problems the public faces, can be utilized once counseling professionals begin to view individuals as living in a constant evolving state of change. This is true of all who set out with a plan to help others overcome personal dilemmas. Some issues we all face can be fleeting, and some require long term monitoring, and recurrent clinical interventions.

Modern day challenges we all face in general are not the chronic obscure dilemmas found among chronic Mental Health patients managing a state of Psychosis, nor the depilating after effects of irreversible brain damage, but the common difficulties we all face through our shared human existence.

Depression hinders ones ability to initiate projects which require motivation, and experiencing anxiety magnifies our perception of fears and in spite of this, it is the author's belief we must despite challenges, continue to strive towards achieving incremental stages of personal growth.

Having a profound compassionate appreciation of underlying dilemmas and devastation Mental Health symptoms can create, the realities of life dictates as humans we all desire a sense of well being. The mind's natural tendency is to resolve conflicts almost as a natural reaction to conflict. When individuals confront obstacles we can either accept the dilemmas and suffer, or wait until conflicts become increasing unmanageable then react. This natural progression towards correcting a problematic situation is innate in all humans. This can be assured as fact, as I have _never_ treated a patient who was happy with their state of discontent, which was interrupted as being a cry for help. Patients ask for an opportunity and a comfortable forum in which to work through their dilemmas, even in the worse case of scenarios. In all the current Psychological literature research will show that those who receive best outcomes from modern Psychotherapy, regardless of discipline, occurs when a patient is in a state of misery.

The patient develops an acute awareness of their current circumstances and its impact. From here, a patient finds the motivation and increased willingness to overcome their current situation and make changes. What has become predictable in this process is patients often come to a realization on their own that avoiding difficult obstacles only compounds the work and effort that will be required from them to resolve the dilemmas if they wait to tackle problems at a later date. An individual state, even after having reached full development, is never stagnant, but ever evolving as a direct result of exposure to life experiences. How life experiences are interpreted impact greatly the development of one's personality style, influencing their unique decision-making abilities, and ability to relate to others constructively. With exposure to complex life experiences difficult to understand at an early age, or developmental trauma, contributes greatly to a failure to adjust later in life. Some would argue the sheer process of *living* fosters challenges and common dilemmas we all must endure. Even the most ordinary of life style has its challenges regardless of social economic status, intelligence level, geography, or cultural affiliation. By virtue of sharing space in civilization is the great equalizer, and as a result, we are never immune from encountering conflict which surfaces from relating with others, even if we give it our best effort to avoid conflict.

Viewing Psychological Growth as available to everyone in society is an easy leap to make if you understand the natural progression theory as stated above, even for the most troubled in our society by Mental Health ailments. Imagine a world in which all of life's unique dynamics we encounter, and behaviors, are reduced into diminutive categories. No human would be immune from finding some condition of normality that applies to them. The longer humans as a species live on this planet, the more advanced we become at categorizing all the conditions we experience in the human existence.

Applause is due for the advances made to date in the field of Clinical Psychology and Psychiatry. As a species, we have explored the depths of Biology; Neurology, the role environment plays on human development, and advances Magnet Resonance Imaging (MRI) technology can provide. MRI technology is a non-intrusive technique for localizing brain lesions and tumors on the human brain. The technology has catapulted us with the ability to analyze visually neurological chemical connections of the brain on a microscopic level very fine about 0.1mm like never before.

Not only can our society now categorize all statistically abnormal symptoms and socially appropriate behavior, we can also categorize statistically significant microbiological discoveries to help describe the human condition.

In the field of professional Clinical Psychology, we have patients who seek treatment for concerns, not deemed clinical, nor chronic or severe, but there are concerns present that influence ones ability to function productively in society, or with loved ones. These concerns are Psychological Social (Psychosocial) Stressors on Axis IV of The American Psychiatric Association *Diagnostic and Statistical Manual of Mental Disorders* Fourth Edition Text Revision (DSM- IV-TR) (2000). The degree to which these stressors affect other areas of one's life will dictate level of significance warranting intervention by the treating Psychologist, or other Health Care Professionals.

Axis IV problems on the DSM-IV-TR include the following titles; Problems With Ones Primary Support Group; Problems Related To The Social Environment; Educational Stressors; Occupational Deficits;

Vocational Or Economic Problems; Problems With Access To Health Care Services; Problems Related To Interaction With The Legal System; and Other Psychosocial And Environmental Problems. These Axis IV problems can be viewed as *a catch all* for anything significant left out of the other categories. In some not for profit institutions, those stressors placed on Axis IV are typically not reimbursable by most major insurance providers, and therefore in order for those Axis IV presenting problems to be addressed exclusively in treatment often falls to the discretion of the facility's management protocol to determine which Psychological Social Stressors warrant clinical care. More often then not, other coexisting problematic symptoms take precedence and the patient will receive treatment for the primary acute symptom even though a Psychosocial Stressor may be viewed as a contributing factor over more intrusive acute symptoms.

The Diagnostic and Statistical Manual of Mental Disorders

The American Psychiatric Association *Diagnostic and Statistical Manual of Mental Disorders* Fourth Edition Text Revision (DSM- IV-TR) (2000) of Psychiatric problems listed by categories, include descriptive symptoms associated with all categories of Mental Illness. It also describes medical conditions and various abusive behaviors that contribute to Mental Health conditions as well as symptom stressors that can be a focus of clinical attention.

Considered the most chronic symptomatic conditions is Schizophrenia in which the person experiences distortions in their perceptions causing hallucinations or delusions. Similar symptoms found in Schizophrenia patients are also often the focus of clinical attention when people abuse or become dependent on illegal drugs and then become psychotic because of their drug use, or when prescription medications reach toxicity levels in patients leading to delirium. The latter is more commonly found in the elderly.

Clinical Depression can be mild forms of sadness, or mood instability, to more severe forms that can manifest into self-harm behaviors. Clinical Depression is not fleeting and does not clear up *"out of the blue."* It requires professional supervision over symptoms. A clinical state of Depression that lasts for more than two years is referred to as Dysthymic Disorder. Forms of Depression with Bipolar states of Depression which include reoccurring cycles of elevated moods of Mania then Depressive states, are also categorized under the umbrella of Depressive Symptoms.

Under this same category of Depression, we also find Adjustment Disorders, which are time limited and Depressive features tend to remit after the stressor is removed, or the patient's situation changes. Problems of Grief & Loss dilemmas, which occur for all of us, fall into this category. Depending on our exposure to an unexpected divorce, change in employment, loss of a significant support structure, position in life, economic status, even the loss of social status due to aging, can also influence ones general ability to adjust and cope with immediate stressors.

Experiencing excessive worry, Panic, Post Traumatic Stress Disorder, or Phobias fall under the category of Anxiety Disorders. Experiencing Social

Anxiety, an inability to feel safe outside of ones home called Agoraphobia, and Obsessive Compulsive Disorders are all under the umbrella of Anxiety. We have varying degrees of anxiety and experiencing mild forms of anxiety in new or unusual situations say in public speaking is normal. When symptoms of Anxiety can be diagnosed as problematic and clinical occurs when symptoms increase and significantly interferes with a person's ability to conduct normal day-to-day functions. Symptoms are debilitating and considered statistically abnormal when one's ability to function, and one's quality of life is significantly reduced in direct result of the amount of time spent managing symptoms of panic or compulsions.

Other categories to include Childhood Disorders, Impulse Control Disorders, Personality Disorders, Family Problems, even Phase of Life Problems are detailed in rich descriptive detail in our current understanding of the popular Diagnostic and Statistical Manual of Mental Disorders (2000). Childhood Disorders include Psychological problems related to behavioral control problems, ADHD, conduct disturbance, and oppositional behavior. Separation anxiety is listed as a common problem in young children. Impulse Control Disorders are considered Psychological problems when they involve a loss of control of Anger and in more severe cases; a diagnosis of Intermittent Explosive Disorder is given in adulthood. Sub categories under the same grouping of disorders include issues of Domestic Violence, Pathological gambling, Kleptomania, Pyromania, and Trichotillomania. General characteristics of all Personality Disorders are summarized with detail given to Obsessive Compulsive Personality Disorders, Narcissistic Personality Disorder, and the elusive Borderline Personality Disorder.

On occasion, an Axis IV diagnosis of Family Problems is assigned when conflicts surface because someone within the family is receiving services to treat their Mental Health Disorder. Alternatively, also mentioned in the DSM is Family Conflicts that often surface and then become Psychological concerns because communication problems, parenting issues, school problems, or sibling conflicts surface as problematic.

Phase of Life conflicts categorized that could warrant Psychological intervention include problems with ageing, career dilemmas, and issues with one's level of life accomplishments. Often the worry is on a lack of accomplishments however the burden of one's over achievement can also bring undue stressors as well as relationship conflicts, stressors related to marriage commitments, and distress due to a lack of commitment in relationships, are all susceptible to the guise of warranting Clinical Psychological intervention.

The American Psychiatric Association *Diagnostic and Statistical Manual of Mental Disorders* Fourth Edition Text Revision (DSM- IV-TR) (2000) is as thorough in its efforts to be descriptive as it is all inclusive of all the problems of living. Over the years, there has been a predictable course of events regarding what can be considered an acute Psychological dilemma for the time. Some disorders listed in the manual are reevaluated for the time period and considered non-clinical, then excluded from the manual while others are deemed problematic and are included in the manual as it undergoes revisions. Over the years, some revisions have occurred in reaction to social pressure and the ever-changing societal standard of what normality is, and how it should be described.

In the preparing of this book, it was important for the author to investigate all aspects of current research documented in the field of Psychology and Psychiatry, and to also investigate what has been neglected in the field and give voice to what has been under emphasized.

Character Strengths and Virtues Handbook

The development of the *Character Strengths and Virtues: A Handbook and Classification* (Peterson & Seligman, 2004), offers an alternative in Psychology to identify and classify the Positive Psychological traits of human beings. Much like the American Psychiatric Association *Diagnostic and Statistical Manual of Mental Disorders* Fourth Edition Text Revision (DSM-IV-TR) (2000) of general Psychological Disorders, the *Character Strengths and Virtues Handbook (CSV)* provides a theoretical framework to assist in developing practical applications for Positive Psychology. This Positive Psychology Psychological Handbook under development identifies six classes of core virtues made up of twenty-four measurable character strengths. The organization of these virtues and strengths is as follows:

1. **Wisdom and Knowledge**: Creativity, Curiosity, Open Mindedness, Love of Learning, Perspective

2. **Courage:** Bravery, Persistence, Integrity, Vitality

3. **Humanity:** Love, Kindness, Social Intelligence

4. **Justice:** Citizenship, Fairness, Leadership

5. **Temperance**: Forgiveness and Mercy, Humility and Modesty, Prudence, Self Regulation

6. **Transcendence:** Appreciation of Beauty and Excellence, Gratitude, Hope, Humor, Spirituality

Use of the Character Strengths and Virtues methods are best used for those seeking to identify individual strengths, and seeking to expand the quality of their lives. This method is not intended for those suffering with chronic Mental Illness. Although this form of progressive systematic research as listed above is not as extensive, nor as established as The American Psychiatric Association DSM, the list of character virtues should not be discounted in its potential value for those more inclined to build upon personal strengths vice the sole focus on those *human nature* characteristics to define and categorize disease.

Psychological Normalcy

Psychological Normalcy is the absence of statistically abnormal symptoms. We all strive to question for ourselves if we are able to adapt and recover from unfavorable circumstances, or the obstacles, which present themselves that may or may not be under our individual control. We live in a society whereby societal norms are often configured not by what is often statistically considered abnormal, but the influence of our own worldview and by the larger culture in which we thrive. As well as by those who in society are willing to persistently challenge accepted truths of the era.

> *Human systems grow in the direction of what they persistently ask questions about.*
>
> *Cooperrider and Whitney*

According to popular beliefs, the term mental and emotional Psychological Normalcy refers to normality in terms of overall health, balance, the absence of any disturbances to interfere with daily functioning. Normality is defined as displaying an average commonly accepted agreed upon response by the society in which one lives in response to life circumstances in comparison to behaviors displayed against the next person in the same given circumstance.

Consensual Validation

Erich Fromm, a Psychoanalyst and Social Philosopher, contends as the field of Psychology attempts to speak of Psychological Normalcy and Mental Health within society the discussion implies a controversial assumption that all societies value the same qualities, and that *human nature* can ever be scientifically statistically validated in the same way. Essentially, he states Psychology can be defined only in terms of the individual's lack of adjustment to the ways of life in his society.

> The approach of normative humanism is based on the assumption that as in the solution of any other question, there are right and wrong, satisfactory and unsatisfactory solutions to the problem of human existence. Mental Health is achieved if man develops into full maturity according to the characteristics and laws of human nature. Mental Illness consists in the failure of such development. What is so deceptive about the state of mind of the members of a society is the consensual validation of their concepts. It is naively assumed that the fact that the majority of people share certain ideas or feelings proves the validity of these ideas and feelings. Nothing is further from the truth. Consensual validation as such has no bearing whatsoever on reason or Mental Health. Just as there is a folie à deux there is a folie à millions. The fact that millions of people share the same vices does not make them virtuous, the fact that they share so many errors does not make the errors to be truths, and the fact that millions of people share the same forms of mental pathology does not make them sane.

> Fromm, 1960

The term Psychological Normalcy, is also compared to the absence of pathology, or any extreme in ones mood, character, and temperament in response to unfavorable circumstances the individual may perceive. From a Humanistic Approach we would define Psychological Normalcy as ideal, or the ability to achieve optimal functioning as referred to in Self Actualization of ones full potential without depilating barriers to hinder future Psychological Growth. Psychological Normalcy is the ability to respond appropriately to events one faces. To implement swiftly adaptive styles of coping in reaction to external or internal situations. In the face of neurological abnormalities, or organic biological influences, we find however, that medical conditions can affect ones ability to function appropriately and maintain what is considered Psychologically Normal. The same is true when artificial biological influences have been introduced in the human system to include either the brief abuse or prolonged dependence on illegal substances, Narcotics, Amphetamines, excessive use of any substance including the abuse of prescription drugs, or over the counter drugs used in excess.

To consider Psychological Normalcy as a process has been proven in the literature as the most varying developmental responses over a lifetime. Periods of isolated decline, or exposure to social stressors, challenge unique coping styles and varying adaptation abilities. Concepts of personal resiliency are important to foster in all stages of development along with knowing individually where one's limits for stress lay.

Achieving and maintaining Psychological Normalcy, or optimal health, entails ones ability to negotiate appropriately conditions of adversity, make individual choices and balance ambivalence as well as balance the expression of warmth, intimacy and humor. The opposite of optimal health is an inability to establish appropriate boundaries with self and others or communicate effectively with others in order to advocate for oneself. In addition, the lack of sustaining focus towards ones passionate desires and harboring a negative worldview for extended periods creates self-generated cynical pessimistic perspectives of ones abilities or environment. This presentation is also likely to impede one's ability to seek assistance when stressors surface. Hence, self-defeating, and is considered most damaging to the individual.

The introverted preference towards ambivalence and feelings of despair mark the defining lines of abnormality in our society that may trigger symptoms of sociopathic behavior, or prolonged periods of statistically abnormal Depressive Mood states, and Psychotic behavioral responses. When combined with parental, or developmental negative influences proven erratic, unresponsive, overly ambivalent, increased interpersonal competencies are lowered even more developmentally in response to those conditions of adverse Psychological predicaments beyond individual control.

Over the years many patients encountered have questioned *Is this normal?* This type of inquiry holds significance as it happens so frequently. I found this to be true if working with patients mandated for treatment and the same line of questioning also occurred if working with well-adjusted college students, or career minded well-adjusted adults in Couples Therapy. To this, I respond with a pause as the stated question always begs for clarification of their unique life dynamics in total that had led to such an inquiry.

The patient's unique life dynamics presented always appear to be void of a clinical presenting problem initially. Underlying their concern however is an irresistible need for reassurance their problems will not linger. The first goal I establish with my patients is to explore their worldview. Then, seek to psychologically empower the patient to be more empowered; take more control over their current situation in diverse times in a creative manner. I ask what would be the first strategy to taking a more pro-active stance in their given predicament. "What would that be for you?" Adopting increased appreciation for their current situation to facilitate adaptive coping skills and strategies to transcend their maladaptive current predicament they may find themselves in is paramount in clinical treatment sessions. Strategies I share with all patients who inquire in such a manner in treatment, regardless if I have clinically analyzed them to have a statistical abnormal, or atypical Psychological response to a life stressor, is to respond with a technique of using Psychological Education.

Surprisingly, this same question *Is this normal?* also arises as frequent in those clients I come across in populations that would be considered normal by both societal norms and Psychologically Clinical standards. The distinction in my clinical approach would be by what means I have encountered such individuals or clients in the public. Even those in society deemed our most *normal* do encounter periods of uncertainty triggering periods of anxiety and distress, and will seek some variation of Psychological expertise to relieve their distress. When attempting to rectify their distressing predicament, many would never consider themselves to be suffering from a statistically abnormal predicament. What I am attempting to make clear is that all individuals will encounter periods of uncertainty, which deplete their reserves of existing templates of life coping skills that has directed them in the past on how to best respond to life stressors. Finally, the realization of the patient is always to question *How Do I?* This is the action phase and the final component in the equation requiring additional leaning, additional Psychological Education to overcome life predicaments.

PART II:

PURSUIT OF FULFILLMENT

CHAPTER THREE

Man's Search For The Meaning Of Life

Everywhere one seeks to produce meaning, to make the world signify, to render it visible. We are not, however, in danger of lacking meaning; quite the contrary, we are gorged with meaning and it is killing us.

Jean Baudrillard

In both Philosophy and Psychology to contemplate the meaning of life remains a central theme along with striving to obtain personal fulfillment. The barriers which surface to obscure this end goal, are often the dilemmas processed in therapy. These complex dilemmas viewed as impeding ones ability to obtain a sense of fulfillment can foster feelings of discontent if one's goal continues to be perceived as unachievable. Conversely, ones level of overall happiness we are finding may have a baseline and pursuing some ultimate goal, when achieved has no guarantee it will manifest more contentment, more joy, or be enough to change ones outlook on life. So then, what gives life ultimate meaning if not the establishment and completion of grand goals?

What we seek above all is a meaningful connection and answers. Philosophy can perhaps facilitate the process for individual contemplation on the mysteries of the universe that ultimately reveals a cohesive framework from which to define one's own sense of meaning. In Psychological research, the field of study can add to society's knowledge base through uncovering commonalities existing in our collective understanding of the truth in human nature, as well as revealing inconsistencies found within those who make up society.

Not being enough, feelings of uncertainty, or the feelings of inadequacy all play a role when traumatic life dilemmas surface. If *Man* is capable of so much good, how can we make sense of acts of evil, which occur, even from good *Men?* Perhaps as a society, we blindly negate this aspect that naturally occurs in all of *Man* with the end result being an intolerance to which we selectively choose to turn a blind eye in ourselves. It is in the author's opinion to contemplate that which is either good or bad is only viewing this dilemma from a one-dimensional perspective. To fully explore this seemingly human common occurrence accurately would be to ask the question of those in society *Why is there so much resistance in accepting Man's proclivity to veer away from ones true character in times of personal devastation? What does it take for Man to restrain themselves from its natural tendency towards negativity we all possess?*

To answer the question *what is the meaning of life?* many have approached the question by examining what is valuable to humans in life. What is it we as humans hold dear and would defend against its lost. Famous Philosophers, Socrates, Plato, Aristotle, Descartes, Spinoza, and many others expressed what was valuable in life was the pursuit of meaningfulness. Aristotle stated the pursuit of happiness was the *Highest Good* and that such is achievable through our uniquely human capacity to.

By contrast, a Nihilistic perspective would argue nothing has value in life. According to Friedrich Nietzsche, Nihilism is characterized as emptying the world and especially human existence of meaning, purpose, comprehensible truth, or essential value.

From a Existential point of view a case is made by 19th century Philosophers Søren Kierkegaard and Arthur Schopenhauer that life can be a leap of faith, full of despair, even quite painful as we experience it, yet despite these naturally occurring realities of life, individuals do find meaningfulness. This is possible if individuals are able to accept themselves unconditionally as they are and by committing themselves to something finite; devoting ones life to a commitment despite the inherent vulnerability of doing so. This perspective is related to taking risks regardless of its outcome and overcoming fear in the pursuit of obtaining something meaningful. Joseph Campbell, Mythologist, Professor, and Author of The *Power of Myth,* during an interview with Public Television's anchor, Bill Moyers, answered the question *what is the meaning of life?* with the following response:

> *People say what we're all seeking is a meaning for life. I don't think that's what we're really seeking. I think what we're seeking is an experience of being alive so that the life experiences that we have on the purely physical plane will have resonances within, that are those of our own innermost being and reality, so that we actually feel the rapture of being alive.*

Much like Existential Philosopher's Kierkegaard and Schopenhauer, Joseph Campbell also shared with his audience a strong theme that life can be full of despair, uncertainty, and doubt, yet to follow ones own path in life is ultimately rewarding. Although it may be a difficult, time ridden journey for many to find their individual path, once discovered, is the most challenging prerequisite of what is required in leading a rewarding life. Once discovered, an individual's level of conviction of character, and drive extended towards meeting their end goals, will influence decisions that will keep them in line with their chosen path. This journey as it were has always been referred to as difficult because as individuals become increasingly exposed to adult realities of life, it can be difficult for most to sustain. Joseph Campbell often referred to this process in what he termed *follow your bliss.* There will never be any guarantees for such a pursuit, but must be approached with a level of certainty and conviction for people to experience the process of following their own path. It is in the initiation of the process and subsequent pursuit; meaning becomes defined for that individual as they participate in the process.

It is a process of sorts. Not the attainment, but the exuberance one extends and subsequent life experiences, in return life rewards us with that which gives life ultimate meaning. Mr. Campbell contends the results of following ones bliss can help define the total fulfillment of who you are, and it may lead you away from fame, away from financial security, or into the lime light. One version to Joseph Campbell's story to illustrate *follow your bliss* includes a slightly different scenario although the overriding meaning remains intact. The setting is of a family at a restaurant. The mother and father are engaged in conversation about the kitchen remodeling project advances back at home and the two children are catching up with the day's events at their High School. The son wants to forgo college and learn a trade. The son interrupts his parents and lets his father in on the big news during dinner. He says, "I have made a decision to travel abroad in Europe and experience life a bit before life becomes too serious." The mother listens carefully and looks to her spouse for his reaction. The father says, "what will you do for money? That's not practical son. I have never done anything I wanted to do in all my life!"

What will the son choose? What decision will have the greatest impact on the man he will become? What will have the greater negative impact, the son denying his desire and curiosity to follow his innate desires to explore, or the decision to comply with his father's wishes against all reason and chance to consider all possible options regarding travel and education?

To impose or to hinder in someway our children's natural curiosities is limiting. Supportiveness can be conveyed by entertaining with children all the possibilities in their current thinking to teach the lesson of reason. Creative thinking teaches us, if a child desires to travel does not necessarily mean they need to travel for a whole year, but perhaps one month of excursion, and then picking up college in the fall when the school year typically commences would satisfy a man's innate hunger to explore. Moreover, would not jeopardize the important father and son relationship the son will need to rely upon once other life challenges present themselves in the future. How we foster relationships along the way is as crucial as the more important topics we will explore in later chapters.

Living up to one's full potential is ranked as a significant component to sustaining happiness. It is said the difference in living ones dream is not the choice we make to achieve our goals even when met with insurmountable odds, but knowing we can do it, and executing it. Following one's bliss as Joseph Campbell intended its meaning is achieving what we are individually meant to do, and doing it once we discover what it is. Can you really pursue Self Actualization and live in a culture that values industry? Does a dichotomy really exist? Most do not need to feel Self Actualized, but we want it.

6*f*

Paradigms

There will always be alternative explanations and varying perceptions to consider from others if we allow ourselves to be open to new *knowledge*. Within this, you may find indistinguishable themes similar to your experiences, or discover new meanings for experiences that have already occurred and come to know it completely anew. To be flexible with discoveries many have concluded allows greater points of view to be explored, and then optimistically we can come to our own conclusions despite the variance that may exist in the literature.

Greek Tragedies, Mythologies, and the literal meanings derived from Western Religion can be for some our most perplexing concepts and area for modern day societies greatest differences. Society's use of paradigms to shape individual meaning is a global commonality we all share. All cultures, over the centuries have developed core paradigms, yet surprisingly this phenomenon occurred simultaneously when the distance of isolation precluded an exchange of ideas. Despite our vast subtle differences found in society, there are far more commonalities we share across cultures. According to Imtiaz Gul (2003),

---

6 *f* Relief depicting Buddha in the garden with Yaksas. Ingo Jezierski, Corbis Photography, Royalty Free (RF) Photography

extraordinary multi ethnic tribes inhabit the Hindu Kush, which cuts through Pakistan, Afghanistan, and Tajikistan. Among them are the reclusive Kalasha tribes believed to be the descendents of Alexander the Great. It is believed they share a common belief earth is the real heaven. They are said to believe that the fruit orchards, waterfalls and the snow melt streams running through the valleys are God's bounty. Not a literal heaven but that earth holds all forms heaven could possess and were meant to be enjoyed by the living.

A popular book *If You Meet The Buddha On The Road, Kill Him! The Pilgrimage Of Psychotherapy Patients,* by Sheldon B. Kopp (1972), is a concept I was introduced to while studying Philosophy and completing a doctoral program in Psychology. When I was introduced to his material previous teachings had no similar concepts to use as reference.

This material was novel and appeared at first glance to be an important enough piece to help clarify what I was also learning about Philosophy and its relation to Psychology. This text sets out to clarify who the Buddha is, what meeting the Buddha implies, and what exactly does killing the Buddha mean metaphorically. On a larger scale, it addresses the question we all come to which is *What Is The Meaning Of Life?*

The title in itself is considered to have shock value I suspect for marketing value in order to jar the reader's curiosity into learning more. The historical Buddha, Shakyamuni, on attaining enlightenment, is said to have realized that all beings, just as they are, are Buddhas. According to the text, if this is so, meeting a Buddha on the road should be a pretty common event as each *individual being* is a Buddha on the road. The context of meeting the Buddha implies encountering something or someone outside of oneself that can supply enlightenment for another. The assertion is that we all have preconceived images and ideals of what a Teacher, or Buddha should look like. As a result, people chase after individuals who seem to live up to our images, and in turn ignore those who do not fit this ideal image. Furthermore, we may even treat ourselves with contempt for not living up to the standards set by our imaginary inner preconceptions.

In considering all hidden meanings or attempting to discount the validity of the claims expressed in the text may keep us pretty busy, but it has nothing to do with real practice, which is an awareness of who and what we actually are, not the pursuit of some idea of who we think we should be. Therefore, "killing the Buddha," means dispelling fantasy images, and "the road" metaphorically is the road outside where we look outside ourselves for the ones who have all the answers. The inner workings of our mind, the road, where we set up all our expectations, or what we must obey to turn ourselves into the Buddha we do not believe we already are, but think we must become. The truth is that no one person is capable of providing all the answers we seek to explain the unexplainable. Even Psychotherapist must be aware of their shortcomings in order to not unknowingly cause undo harm to their patients.

Life is both short, unfair, and there is no good justification why we as humans do not get all that we desire. Our only one mild assurance to get what we desire in life is to have a willingness to be a curious thinker about the world in which we live in. It is said that Shakyamuni's last dying words to his disciples were, "Be a lamp unto yourselves." Be your own light, your own authority, your own Buddha. Kill off every image of the Buddha, see who and what you are in this very moment, and see that there is no Buddha other than this moment.

The choice to deduct meaning from this unique perspective explained rests on the reader. If we only take the saying *If You See A Buddha On The Road, Kill Him* to mean only that we should reject all forms of external authority, we will end up leaving ourselves at the mercy of all sorts of other unconscious, inner *Buddhas*. This can be dangerous for the self-centered narcissist. Our Psychological reality is that we have to learn and practice to achieve our independence, and that learning almost inevitably has to take place within the context of some kind of disciplined practice. Some form of container with professional ethical boundaries we establish for ourselves. Teachers come in many forms. The patience we learn from a random act or from the lesson of forgiveness can be a form of teaching. Finding the inner strength to believe in oneself and continue a personal commitment to improve ones character is important as well.

Imagine now your most prominent image of greatness, a spiritual leader, or an image of something or someone who you admire for their great achievements.

Most likely, a human image manifests. To take it a step further, think of all the millstones this person has accomplished, and what this person is best known for. Now, make a list of what personal characteristics and values a person such as this would have to possess to achieve all they have accomplished. If the inner Buddha in you possessed only a third of those qualities, or committed to a process to practice those qualities in your daily living, how would the quality of your life improve?

The Secret To Life

The secret to life is, you. Efforts involved in finding the secret to life have been explored in obscure beliefs, historical Philosophical truths, and scientific efforts to uncover a single truth that connects us all to explain human existence. To define truth, scientist claim the secret to life is within ones DNA. Concepts of searching for ones core motivations and meaning hold similarities across time, but not in all domains of investigation, or in what we in society value or perceive about their unique existence. Across all subsets of religion, race, culture, geography, phases of life, and even within eras in history, we find differences among those in society.

The single most common dominator we have for measuring the secret to life is in knowing you are alive and what choices one will make to live their life in the time they have left.

One rational in this thinking is to reference Plato's contention that *love* is a universal common occurrence we all share, but it is not consistently expressed in the same way across all those in human existence. A person's capacity to value the benefits of love for self and others is universal and can be expressed in vastly different pursuits. If love was pure, the one common dominator, and unadulterated, then why is love pursed in less than virtuous ways? There are those who have a deep, often excessive inappropriate love for things, drugs, pornography, or the elusive obsessive pursuit for wealth above all others. When you find love though, how does anyone ever know it will survive the test of time? There is no certainty. When it does, most would say, "you're lucky!" Love is for the lucky. Moreover, we know from the benefit of time, it is not just for the lucky; Love is for those who welcome it into their lives. We also know that with time, beauty can and does fade, so then one is left with the individual they have pursued. Many have argued then if love is enough to sustain us.

Know thyself fully. In my career, I have advocated that the single most important goal in all the therapy I have provided to patients is to convey the importance of knowing themselves first before other matters could be attended to with full commitment. If a patient got nothing else from my teachings is that they at least give themselves the opportunity to explore their individual boundaries, share what is the most difficult and gave themselves the benefit of telling their unique story to others. This is the crust of Professional Therapy. The superficial layer of one's defense mechanisms being unfolded for review and presented for criticism even perhaps receiving positive validation, which allows for an individual to be known by others. What I am attempting to convey here is the importance of allowing others to observe that part of you that is alive, that part of you that strives for more, regardless of the challenges, or what has not materialized yet, is the essence of you. Beautiful and full of potential. Give yourself no less than the best in you. Be known.

The Myth of Spirituality

Spirituality is not a religious conversion. When we speak of *Spirituality* know that we are not talking about Religion. It is ok to keep the two divided at this part of our learning curve. We can give ourselves permission to explore new perspectives on Spirituality perhaps never considered before without threatening one's established sense of religious faith. Spirituality can be defined as a means of sustaining sanity and Psychological health. The focus of spirituality is how individuals experience life, their unique human personal experience in daily living. In the practice of incorporating concepts found in spirituality promotes greater appreciation of one's life and the lives of others.

Throughout time *Man* has sought to answer many of life's most intriguing questions. Chiefly, the question *What Is The Meaning Of Life?* What Is My Purpose? *How Do We Know If We Are Living Up To Our Full Potential? What Is Happiness?*

In history, a shifting occurred between organized religion, and Philosophical beliefs that would later contribute greatly to modern man's concept of Spirituality. In this section, we will explore both fact and fiction on the topic of Spirituality as well as our inconclusive understanding of the body and mind debate. We study spirituality and Philosophy, in hopes of coming to our own individual conclusions of what would be best for us regarding one's life purpose, achieving a sense of connection with something greater than self, values clarification, and personal ethics. Spirituality teaches us life lessons similar to that found in religion, yet uniquely different because spirituality does not dictate, nor attempt to regulate that which is innate in all people, or what people are capable of deducting on their own without the need for another's human analytical filter. Spirituality is an ever-changing process of enjoying ones own human existence unique to the individual.

First, Spirituality is not a religious conversion. To become a spiritual person does not mean the person is struck by a thunderbolt of lighting from a supernatural mythological heaven, and is then magically transformed into a different person. Nor is becoming more spiritual a forced conversion that magically pressures people to become all consumed in an obsessive manner with mythical characters, nor is it a push to explore further than you would typically into theories found in historical Church Scriptures. This is divinely different, and unique. This has more to do with one's own character vice theological history when we speak of Spirituality. Becoming more *Spiritual* is increasing ones awareness of ones deepest identity, which is already there, perhaps not enlightened and empowered.

Many people may have very deep rooted, logical, and concrete definitions of what spiritual is in which the term God takes center stage from which all references are made. Regardless of your present personal definition of religion, the purpose of this chapter is not intended to challenge this. This chapter is not intended to be a reference for religious teachings, nor is it speaking as an authority on religion. This chapter is not intended to define, or to redefine your current understanding of religion, as we will not be discussing religion. Religion is faith, a belief, or level of faith conviction. It is ok to keep the two, Spirituality and Religion, separate for our present purposes.

It is the author's contention that all people are free to believe what they choose, or to worship in any form they deem appropriate for them. My career in Psychology has allowed me access to patients each with unique defense mechanisms they use to guard against the realities of life. I would go as far to say those with both traditional and nontraditional ideas of faith all possessed a depth of curiosity to explore alternatives that can enhance the quality of their life only because their current understanding of life simply was not effective and quite frankly, often confusing for the individual. Gaining knowledge beyond traditional learning templates is what I find in my practice most seek. An expanding upon what is already there. Essentially, it is a mild shifting of ones level of willingness to self explore, to enhance their experience of day-to-day living.

Being spiritual is not that you have everything together. According to Hazelton, a premier rehabilitation treatment center on the East Coast, being spiritual is a glimpse into something new. It is an opening to something unexplored which may lead to something more fulfilling. It is an opening of the eyes to new values, that will ultimately influence ones attitude and it starts a process, which may take you on a new life path.

Exploring *Spirituality* enables individuals to begin understanding and clarifying their values. In Psychology, it is similar to gaining new insights about oneself, which will ultimately greatly affect future decision-making abilities and behavior.

It is roughly a moving from a state of distortions into more grounded states of reality for ones Psychological well being. The process is a moving from dishonesty into honesty, from distrust of oneself or others into becoming a more trusting individual. It also allows individuals to move away from leading a chaotic lifestyle into one with clarity by examining ones values. The person can then choose whether to accept new values based on insight because they understand the full weight of doing so, and not just complying for the sake of random change.

A New Insight --------------- → Moving Towards -------- → Not Just Comply

Distortion .... Moving Towards .... Reality
Dishonesty .... Moving Towards .... Honesty
Distrust .... Moving Towards .... Trusting
Disintegration/Insanity .... Moving Towards .... Integration/Clarity
False Pride .... Moving Towards .... Humility

Living a life with humility begs the question what would it take to let others help? You get a sense that you cannot do it by yourself. An example of this is the plight of the illegal drug abuser. An addict is a person by all clinical definitions is one that uses illegal drugs in excess leading to self-destruction, and has attempted to quit drugs with no success. In this example, the addict develops a mindset that "I can do it alone." This person's value system surrounding self sufficiency and what defines his value as a human, convinces him that in order for them to portray strength, he must hold on to his sense of pride and prevail even in situations that exceed his current skill level. This is False Pride.

His *False Pride* convinces him "I can do it by myself without help or support." The *False Pride* responds to its external critics when they point out to the person how destructive their drug use has become and the *False Pride* responds, "Don't listen to them! I have this under control."

When in fact the drug addiction has consumed every aspect of their existence and the end results, which everyone on the outside can clearly see as immensely damaging, the addict's reality remains distorted concerning how large a negative impact their drug use is making. The addict believes everything is under control and may even feel threatened if an outsider attempts to challenge their perception of their circumstances. In this example, increased humility is needed by the person abusing drugs in order to feel okay about allowing outside support, and a shifting away from believing they must always have all the answers.

Allowing help from others is never a personal failure, but some may perceive it as such.

This Psychological dynamics can also be seen in the plight of the divorcee whose life unravels after a realization greater independence and courage will be required of them post divorce. Anytime we exceed our current skill set to resolve unexpected life situations does not mean we are faulty, or any less self-sufficient. What this equates to is in life we are all subjected to happenstance; periods in our life we will have to endure a new situation life has not yet prepared us for, yet we must overcome it.

Typically, when approaching a new life situation we have never experienced before, or the learning of a new trade, we ask for help, seek out new knowledge. We do not unnecessarily place undue burden or guilt on ourselves for not knowing how to maneuver a new skill set we have had no reference for. Ultimately, there are no particular reasons why we lose out on some things, but when these unfortunate situations occur we must take personal responsibility over our hardships to do your best nonetheless.

Rugged Individualism

Rugged individualism means that some people begin to believe they must go it alone. They in essence become an island onto themselves. You have heard the song before with the lyrics *I am a rock, I am an Island.* Adopting a rigid sense of self has its consequences as it can lead to isolation so that no one gets in and no one is allowed out. Who wants to be powerless, but in several ways many of us know we are powerless to a lot of life situations we must endure over the course of a lifetime. In addition, in spite of this disheartening realization, continue to preserver and live a life of meaning.

Spirituality is the willingness to participate in an on-going process of individual exploration that will allow the individual to arrive at a vantage point of knowing who they are and what they value. With more insight, we can make changes to improve upon what already exists.

Spirituality teaches us to be humble. The practicing of humility is not that a person becomes subservient to others or is always placed in a role to acquiescent when confronted by others, but arrives at a state of being that they can now practice controlled strength or power. The controlled person knows what they need and want, and adopts a belief they cannot always do things on their own without some form of support, mentoring, or professional partnerships. They are at ease with themselves. We can actually see and feel how less a role feeling anxiety play in their lives as they are able to not only accept themselves fully, but to quickly set others at ease.

They do not use differences to evaluate the quality of an individual, but strives to focus on other's strengths and possess a wonderful accessibility. Not fear. There is also a lesser importance placed on a need to control. Their friendships are with other people, other human beings and not with self-destructive situations, chemicals, drugs, or hidden agendas to manipulate others in a negative way.

The basic fundamentals of *Spirituality* teach us that making progress is more important than striving to be perfect. Progress is not perfection. Besides, being perfect is not possible and if it were, it would be extremely boring for others to be around.

What Does Spirituality Mean To Me?

To be spiritual is what to me now based on my individual understanding of Spirituality? _____

_____

_____

_____

_____

To be truly human means what to me now based on my current understanding of the human experience?

_____

_____

_____

_____

_____

My Dream My Nightmare

Life contains but two tragedies. One is not to get your heart's desire; the other is to get it.

Socrates

In all the striving we do as unique and separate individuals, we all have a common striving to achieve some sense of accomplishment whatever that may be for the individual. No matter what our individual goals may be, we instinctually always think our predicament is unique and unlike anyone else's experience when in fact they are all the same, just in varying degrees. We may have accomplished something superiorly grand in our lifetime, yet continue to downplay what it has cost us to achieve it. All the while, the next person sits in great contemplation and appreciation in hopes of achieving perhaps only a third of what the person in front of them has achieved. This is termed *My Worst Day Is Someone Else's Dream* Syndrome.

We underestimate our own accomplishments and may even become side tracked into believing we are not enough once we have mastered a sense of accomplishment. Even our most disadvantaged in society has much to be appreciative for. Basic survival is innate in all of us and should never be marginalized. The Human Spirit has proven it can persevere through extreme deprivation, extreme restrictions to its sense of basic freedoms afforded all, and has proven its remarkable abilities to muster courage in light of insurmountable odds. Still, we have the question at hand. What to empower and what to criticize a given individual for *not being enough*. It is all enough. We are all enough just as we are.

The next step is to question and process what patterns make us feel uniquely frustrated.
- Conflicts
- Not getting needs met
- People not responding quick enough
- Unfair situations

We next explore what patterns make us feel fulfilled.
- Feeling a sense of accomplishment
- Feeling connected with a shared purpose with others

- Actions initiated and what is keeping them from taking more decisive actions towards an end goal they state is important to feeling more fulfilled

Therein lays the great dilemmas for all. Getting to the obstacles is the next layer below the surface of any great intervention but requires trust and a non-judgmental element on the part of the person processing the obstacles. People desire to be inspired. Not by the over processing of what has occurred that got them to their current predicament, but new learning that will bring out the best in them as individuals. True lasting change does not occur in a vacuum and what I seek with patient's is not a superficial change for the sake of change, but rather for patient's to explore and discover in themselves their own compelling reasons to take decisive actions towards helping themselves past troubling conflicts they endure.

In my profession as a Psychologist, there are self-proclaimed scientists who will examine the nuances of a symptom, and there are skilled technicians who seek to uncover the underlying dynamics that contribute most to self-defeating patterns of behavior in need of adjustment. The successful ones in practice have learned the art of seeing the value in the patient discovering for themselves the compelling reasons to foster lasting change. Not just a carefully crafted maneuvering of a patient's belief about their predicament, but the Psychologist harbors a mindset to allow its patients the space and time in which to foster compelling reasons why they must change for themselves. For lasting change to occur, overtime, the patient must be self-motivated to make adjustments. If the change is superficial and compelling reasons are not committed to, any changes that occur will only be short lived once motivation levels dwindle with time. So, what gets in the way to presenting such a carefully crafted skill in my techniques? Obstacles of time. We all want to be enough for ourselves and if motivation levels are not initially high enough, the author contends spending more time finding compelling reasons for the patient until the best can be brought out in them. It is there we give more time to uncover their personal best. If we reach this point in the therapy process we don't cheat the patient by giving up but struggle with them through the pain staking current dilemmas until a compelling reason can be uncovered by the patient.

Effort and results manifest the life we design. Anyone who tells you other wise are entitled to their opinion and may have never given themselves the opportunity to explore beyond conceivable personal boundaries of success. Remember it takes risk and conquering fear to achieve such transformations with patients. Not the listening to a voice that tells you what you want most to pursue is beyond obtaining. When we encounter obstacles, the condition can be either a depilating circumstance that influences every aspect of ones existence, or can be described as a minor normal temporary inconvenient stressor to address leaving the inflicted free to move on with life once the stressor has subsided.

That is until the next stressor appears. In life, we are all unique yet share many variables in common. We all have dilemmas, just different dilemmas at different times in our life, which are ever changing.

CHAPTER FOUR

Everyone Wins At The Basics

*I*n life there is one race no one loses. Everyone will win at the basics and reach the final stages in the game of life. This is certain. Ultimately, it is just a matter of time we all reach our demise, and then it becomes a question of how well one wishes to win the game of life. If you have not yet had an opportunity to contemplate this dilemma, you will. Someone should tell us from the start we have only a limited time in which to live. Not only that life is short, but our time is extremely limited in which to construct a quality life we most desire. One in which you desire it to be, complete, fulfilling, and meaningful to the individual.

Someone should tell us from the very beginning that your days are limited, and if there is anything you secretly desire to accomplish in your short existence, do it now as there will never be a more opportunistic moment than now. Do it now. I would encourage people not to focus on what you may have not yet accomplished, but rather to give oneself permission to contemplate what is left before you in the future to accomplish. Then, decide in advance what is needed to make it a reality in each and every day. Develop a comprehensive plan, and then share your strategy with others. Implement it. Evaluate your results, then revisit the strategy and fine tune it along the way. Not just once, but continue to evaluate your successes and obstacles in order to really make your life the one you desire by design.

The greatest failure of most people is that they fail at the execution and implementation phase of their life goals. Look at any basic business model and the evidence will prove that many fail in their ability to be successful in their implementation of goals. They fail not because they lack a clear vision, or a sound business plan, but they fail because they lack the necessary skills of implementation and sustainability overtime. The true test and measure of ones success is in ones ability to successfully develop a winning idea, develop a plan, implement a strategy, launch the product, then re-evaluate over and over again what is working and identify obstacles. A successful businessperson will make necessary corrections as needed and stay the course no matter what it takes. This personal failure of most is not a matter of limited reserves in motivation levels it is a question of tenacity.

Tenacity takes both a clear conviction to the vision and character. Just at the breaking point where most would give up at surmounting demands, those with a strong character and sense of conviction will always stay the course despite minor set backs. It's a learning curve. Once a person is able to maneuver past this stage, they may obtain some success and gain the confidence to repeat the pattern. With time the periods of success become growingly more frequent and convince the person, yes they can do it based on their track record, but if a person gives up too early they will never learn this very important basic lesson I am trying to convey here.

In the book *Sacred Wounds Succeeding Because Of Life's Pain*, by Jan Goldstein (2003), he explains the story of the young, untested sailor, experiencing the sea for the first time and learning his first lesson of how important it is to modulate our natural reactions to fear based on reality and not misperceptions of reality.

Think of a novice sailor who has never had experience at sea. He goes out with a seasoned caption and several accomplished seaman on a sporting expedition. En route, he becomes alarmed at the growing convergence of gray clouds on the horizon. Suddenly, there's a bolt of lightning thrown into the mix. By now he's shaking with fear, warning the captain that they had better turn back or risk being lost out in the massive sea. As the young sailor continues to scan the darkness in the cloud formations and notes several more lightning bolts, he works himself up into a state of frenzy. The captain smiles gently and pulls him aside. Those clouds are moving in a southwest direction. Floaters, we call them. Sporadic lightning often accompanies them; we've seen it many times. A true storm would spread out north and west as well – this is a small pattern. Trust me, we're fine.

(Goldstein, 2003)

83

The lesson Goldstein emphasizes is that what we view initially as violent storms on the horizon and all the emotional unrest it can generate, are easy to overcome if we use new skills, the basic skill of Cognitive Reframing to turn an impossible situation into something manageable and positive. Consequently, in the same way a new life experience can be challenging to overcome with limited skill and knowledge, the same is true in attempting to understand what previous life pains a person may have endured. For example, if a person has only experienced pain in relationships it would stand to reason that one's natural tendency will be to avoid relationships at all cost because they have equated *all* relationships are painful. If we later challenge this perspective and factor in a new understanding that relationships are by design meant to have periods of pain, discomfort, and overcoming this aspect of a relationships natural course is relatively simple, perhaps the person develops new insight and would welcome new relationship opportunities in the future.

What Is Life Meant To Be?

Is life enjoyed most by the ambitious? Or, is life a mere sequence of happenstance? For those in life who show initiative and question what they want out of life, are they happier? Is one's quality of life even meant to be questioned or to be curious about? These are not questions easily answered, nor are they easily answered without some individual contemplation at every phase of ones development. The answers to these questions posed are *Yes*.

> *There will never be a perfect time or a more opportunistic break in the schedule to position you to take action. Now is the time to take action.*
>
> *Dr. Lofton*

If you believe you can do more, you should now. Learning how to incorporate a sense of Spirituality into daily living has significant benefits in helping people discover what is most important to them. As humans, we have a predetermined time on earth in which to enjoy the full range of both real phenomena life has to offer, and to enjoy the self-manufactured aspects available. The latter are the superficial things in life people manufacture for themselves to achieve a sense of happiness. Their effects are however consistently unfulfilling over time for those who pursue them. Listing them is fruitless as they are as varied as people are. The most popular ones are achieving a sense of importance from ones employment title as a substitute to gaining the respect of others through ones generosity and being a kind and loving person. They believe that ones possessions are more important than investing emotionally in a real person.

Many popular movies depict similar themes of choice and superficiality. The theme of a woman being left to her work, and she equates this to being an adequate state of existence is a popular example. In the movie *Reds*, with Warren Beatty and Diane Keaton, the audience is afforded but a brief glimpse into this dynamics at play. Diane Keaton's character is a radical American journalist involved with the Communist revolution in Russia, but by choice wonders seemingly aimlessly to document the greatest story of her encounters, yet reaches a threshold when encountered by Warren Beatty's character who offers her more in the form of being *wanted*. Beyond her full concentrated focus on writing and self identified role as a journalist to sustain a identify for herself, her character becomes transformed. Diane Keaton's character needs and desires appear to shift.

In reality, this choice is only by default of circumstances that she gains more meaning through work and not more meaningful connections with others after we see when she encounters a worthy partner who will offer more meaning than ever before obtained through work efforts. She begins to question if the end result of her life choices are now enough. If she wants more, then it becomes painful to contemplate if wanting more than she has experienced before in the past is important enough to pursue in the future.

In a historically popular movie in North America written by Herman J. Mankiewicz and directed by Orson Welles (1941) a complex character by the name of Charles Foster Kane is depicted from his early youth to his final death in the movie *Citizen Kane*. This movie has been noted as being the best movie of all time and agreeably the most difficult to decipher its ending. In the movie the viewer is lead by the work of a character Thompson, an investigative journalist, seeking to discover the meaning of Charles Foster Kane's dying word: *Rosebud*, and so is often presented as a mystery. The character Thompson, serves a role of both narrator of the film and voice for the audience in understating the meaning of Charles Foster Kane's life.

The movie is also regarded by many as a thinly disguised narration of the life of media magnate Randolph Hearst. The movie explores concepts of power by focusing on the way in which one man gained and maintained economic, social, and political influence through the expansion of his business empire. The title *Citizen Kane* is deemed ironic, as Charles Kane, being wealthy and powerful, was not considered a citizen of the nation in any ordinary sense. He often attempts to manipulate the attitudes and values of ordinary citizens through the content of his newspapers in a destructive way which would be considered in modern times as an abuse of power for self gain and opprobrium.

Charles Kane's empire held over thirty-seven newspapers, thirteen magazines, and a radio network. His empire was considered an empire upon an empire. Charles Kane established grocery stores, paper mills, apartment buildings, factories, forest developments for profit, gold mines, and ocean liners. Charles Foster Kane was a man who got everything he wanted, and then lost his wealth. In the movie, the character was depicted to be a man of incredible wealth, influence, and experienced a string of superficial relationships whom none could satisfy his longing for what was lost in his youth when he was taken from his biological parents. In the beginning of the movie we see a young Charles playing on his snow sled just as authorities, in a most dramatic way, abduct him from his parent's home. In the close of the movie, a large furnace, with an open door, dominates the scene. Workers are discarding all of Kane's accumulated luxuries, paintings, and statues, thrown into the flames, including a weathered snow sled with the words *Rosebud* painted across it.

The reporter, Thompson, feels that what the word *Rosebud* signifies will remain a mystery; a piece of a puzzle to understand the character of the man. The audience is led to believe the sled probably doesn't explain much of anything, but holds significant meaning in that only the movie audience is left to decipher the totality of the life of Charles Foster Kane in true film characterization as only Orson Wells could depict.

For this author, *Rosebud*, the name on the snow sled represents what Kane lost in his youth. A chance at experiencing intimacy lost, that Kane could not recapture with others despite his accumulation of wealth and influence in his lifetime. Each individual chooses over the course of one's lifetime what will have more meaning and importance to him or her. This is uniquely a choice made by billions daily. I speak to you of something at this portion of our journey together which is the less complicated part of life. I trust those things one can receive and feel deep affection for will guide your choices.

Finding Spirituality in daily life is often viewed as the elusive, but in reality is the most accessible on a daily basis once it has been deemed important and of value to an individual. Choosing to be a loving person vice placing more value on ones material possessions is the daily challenge. There will always be enough for all of us if we adopt this simple spiritual perspective. I speak of truths in this lifetime. Some things are a matter of fact in this lifetime and others are conjecture.

Over the centuries not much has changed despite ones geography in the world, culture, or the test of time. There are basic truths that reoccur through time measurable only with time and not always observable in the moment. It's like that mush you see in the stove that when you stare at it for so long waiting for it to change, it just stays the same. However, give it an hour or so and you check on it again and fortunately it has changed form into something edible. Elapsed time was the important component. Over time we manufacture new meanings as a society as well. Present day has led us to be more cognizant of others, and of living more meaningful lives based on a fundamental appreciation for others.

Moreover, in the end it is not the utility bill we will ponder whether we paid it on time or not. At the end of my short life I will be reminded most of the people in my life that have helped shaped my life. I will be reminded of the memories from relationships I enjoyed the most. The people in my life that have so graciously loved me, and those I allowed myself to love. So few I must admit, but perhaps by design I had the privilege to experience something so awe inspiring, so rare. For that single accomplishment in my life I am fortunate to have experienced at all.

A popular Scottish Proverb teaches us to be happy while you are living because when you die, you will be dead for a very long time. From an unsuspecting source, I learned an important lesson I will never forget. The Cancer diagnosis was made and confirmed. There was no disputing the finality of its course and I wanted to help a patient in need as a compassionate Psychologist. I wanted to help this patient process his news and assist him in making sense of what it may mean to him. Our entire session was spent processing stories of his earlier days of loved ones from the past. I felt connected to him in a way I had not felt before in previous sessions and remember feeling concerned about his history of not reaching out to others may limit him gaining support from others when he needed it most as his disease progressed. I felt connected to him in a way I had not felt before in previous sessions and remember feeling concerned about his history of not reaching out to others may limit him gaining support from others when he needed it most as his disease progressed. He was a proud independent man who was self-sufficient and relied on only himself. At least that was his history. Our session ended with him thanking me for my time spent with him, which was the customary way all our sessions ended.

I personally felt compelled to support him in anyway I could as his Therapist. The next session he did not show. I later learned that the previous night, he cleaned his room, socialized in the day room with associates also in the inpatient program, he individually thanked his staff for their help. One Staff commented how she did not think much of his conversations, as he was always respectful and appreciative. He thanked her for how nice she was in the morning when he came down to sign out supplies, or an iron. That evening after he had thanked individually all the people that extended unconditional care to him in the residence, he turned in his key at the front desk and proudly walked out the front door. No mention as to where he was headed. In my thoughts I knew. He went to see about a companion in a neighboring State. By his history and limited access to funds, he probably walked and hitch hiked the entire way to spend his remaining days with the one he loved in a meaningful way. I was sad that I had not had an opportunity to wish him well. Nevertheless, I was also reminded of what is important and what the human spirit will do when they find what has ultimate value in life; that something that is meaningful to them. They change. They choose to make choices that perhaps in the past were not important. The lessons I learned is that in the end it is not a matter of what you have, you ask only two very important questions of one self; who loved me, and who did I allow myself to love. This is all that matters.

Illness is the ultimate test of the human spirit. We connect differently because we see the whole picture and its finality. The mystery is removed. There is nothing to filter the illusion of time. There is nothing to distract us from taking action because a person has no choice but to see reality as it really is. Negative news can come almost like a jolt to the senses to bring into clarity the importance of taking action on that we deem the most important. A heightened sense of awareness is what many describe it as.

Why is it only during these times we experience such clarity? Can we predict why some people give into defeat, while others when faced with a life-altering dilemma seem to become more energized and make life-altering decisions? It is a mystery of life. If you knew what those important qualities are, would it make a difference to how you are leading your life now?

You would get going right? Or, would you wait for things to get really bad before you took action? This is just hypothetical so there is no true measure how a person will respond to adversity, but we do know part of the dilemma now and have the benefit of truth to guide us in the decisions we make in this lifetime.

The game of life will eventually come to an end. It is just a matter of time. If you find this too depressing to contemplate now, then perhaps the harshness of life has not yet thumped you to your core, or perhaps you have not experienced the crushing effects of losing a loved one. You will. Give it time. Everyone will experience it at one point in their lifetime. The magic lies in how we recover from adversity. Once we become aware of how precious life is we no longer value trivial things, the quest to pursue negative influences over others, nor situations that squander the preciousness of life. Those who develop an appreciation of life no longer waste time on negative behaviors, nor participate in unnecessary arguing, or sharing negative words that only foster more negativity.

Everyone says, *How the time flies.* The days go by, then years, and before you know it, we are faced with a state of being which is finally our whole life, and we are left with only memories. Each daily portion can be wasted, or it can be a pleasure, before it is gone forever. If a bedtime review of the day concludes that we were too stressed, too busy, didn't accomplish anything, didn't have any fun, then it has been another lost piece of precious life. Perhaps we are putting off our enjoyment until we have more time, more money, or some other improved situation. The trouble with this is a perceived improved situation may never happen, or it may be too long in coming. It is so important to accept this time, this very minute, as something of tremendous value that will very soon be gone forever. There are many ways to ensure we make the best of our time here on earth. In our daily routine let's include time to enjoy others and ourselves. Look around you. Really see and ponder the wonder of nature. To ponder the simplicity found in nature offers the observer not only tranquility, restful moments in which to reflect, but an appreciation of ones own significance in the world.

89

Humans are small by comparison to nature but significant non the less in the larger scheme of life. In addition, each small significant life contributes to the larger picture beyond and external to ones human existence.

Children at play marvel in the wonders of nature that often inevitability restores their innate nature to folic, dance lightly, and to celebrate their very basic naiveté understanding of just being alive. Adults too, if given the time to restore themselves in a beneficial manner of their choosing, also report rejuvenating results. It is a standard practice in many Personal Growth Retreats to request of the Adults to contemplate the magnitude of the world in which they thrive and how nature is so spectacular. Adult Personal Growth Retreat participants are often provided exercises to contemplate how nature can rejuvenate itself effortlessly. Even instructed to purposely sit at the ocean's edge or go scuba diving and ponder the resilience of oneself. The human body is also a marvel of nature, which continues to rejuvenate itself with little effort. The human body is a highly engineered sophisticated machine built for greatness often though we as Adults become so consumed with the tasks of daily living we forget the simple lessons such exercises can produce.

> *This world, after all our science and sciences, is still a miracle; wonderful, magical and more, to whosoever will think of it.*
>
> *Thomas Carlyle*

A few more things we can do to ensure we make the best of our time here on earth is to face our problems bravely, confidently, and improve on your situation, no matter what state it may be in today. Express acts of goodness to garner its subsequent individual rewards. Be active and improve your mind. Contribute. Laugh, relax, and sleep well is my prescription for leading a fulfilling life.

Those who reach a level beyond *The Basics* are not only willing to make difficult decisions and tackle dilemmas, which confront them; they display a high willingness to take action when needed. We also find those individuals have adopted a powerful mindset that propels them to take action. In contrast, what impedes Psychological Growth is discussing something outside of ourselves, something far away instead of addressing conflicts we are faced with. Yes, they may question what is not working in their lives, yet find little motivation to change it. When faced with critical issues to resolve, everything seems thorny and taking action is never executed.

What I mean by this is that at every stage of your life you may find yourself in conflict when you face a dilemma. The dilemma is such that you must decide among only two choices. It is either or. Dilemmas are something where you must choose. Like being pregnant you are, or you are not. If you don't decide nature takes its course and a decision is made for you. You see with a dilemma you chose option one or two. There is a third option to not choose, but in not choosing someone else chooses for you by default and always proves to be less empowering and ultimately self defeating for the individual.

In 1996, I devised an exercise termed *The Chapters of My Life* (Lofton, 1996), a self-reflective exercise, which would allow participants to reveal and discuss intimate topics about their lives, they would not normally reveal. The design is an original exercise based on my work with Psychological Growth Retreats. It is an autobiographical approach used to obtain as much personal information on each individual. I had a hypothesis that there were but a few life issues we all have in common.

In the field of Professional Psychology we find a patient's ability to self disclose is a key component in problem resolution. The difficulty is that it is also the core hurdle in most therapy sessions for Counselors to arrive at a place where patients feel comfortable enough to disclose. *The Chapters of My Life* exercise is a self-reflective exercise, which allows participates to understand how they react to revealing Stage of Development topics with a stranger. The exercise is presented as a self-disclosure exercise and opportunity to help participants identify what they want most.

For the exercise, participants are provided an exercise form that lists specific age groups. The person assigns a Chapter Title for each age group, then ranks the level of affect this event impacts their life present day.

The Chapters of My Life

Instructions: Fill in a title for each chapter of your life. Write a title that best describes an event, situation, feeling, or a turning point in your life during each age group. Then, place an (X) to the right hand side to indicate the level of effect this age group influenced the shaping of the individual you are today.

Age	Chapter Title	Level of Effect on Your life Today
		Slight Impact....+....+....+....Great Influence
0-5		
6-10		
11-16		
17-20		
21-25		
26-30		
31-35		
36-42		
43-52		
53-62		
63+		

Life Issue: _____

For the purpose of clarity in identifying the two subjects involved, the first participant is called Facilitator and the second participant is referred to as Subject.

The Facilitator reviews the form completed by the Subject and determines if the most significant event falls into one of the following categories to include: Anxiety, Self Defeating Patterns, Low Self Esteem, Loneliness, Intimacy, Sexuality, Family Pressures, Work Related Problems, Separation and Divorce, Loss of Loved Ones, Life Transitions, Values Clarification, Goal Setting, or Increasing Creativity.

The Facilitator when given the completed exercise form, looks for the Chapter which was most effected. This person states "Tell me what you would write about in this Chapter?"

The Facilitator allows two minutes for the Subject to respond. The Facilitator does not speak, ask questions, or give advice. When the two minutes are up the Facilitator will respond to what the Subject shared by stating:

"When you shared _____ it made my think of a similar experience in my own life. I was _____ years old and _____. It influenced who I am today because I learned _____. "

The Facilitator describes a similar experience unique to their own life to the Subject or how what the Subject shared make them think of and how their experience has effected the person they have become.

The Facilitator then assigns a Life Issue from the available list of issues to the Subject's *Chapters of My Life* exercise and then writes it on the bottom of the exercise form. Facilitators are ask to choose only from the provided list of fourteen issues.

As a debriefing to the exercise Facilitators and Subjects were ask by myself how comfortable they felt discussing personal issues with someone they hardly knew. For participants who completed the exercise and were Mental Health Therapists, they were ask; How might you make clients feel more comfortable sharing their deepest concerns in their life?

As a Therapist I often have difficulty dealing with _____ in my own life? Did you have similar issues as your Subjects? Perhaps still remain affected by an issue similar to your Subject, or has been one of your issues in the past?

Results for *The Chapters of My Life* exercise was a confirmation my hypothesis was true and that The Wounded Therapist concept is true. It is very difficult for Counselors to work through and accept their own pain and problems. From the general list of Life Issues given to include Anxiety, Self Defeating Behavior, etc., helps to prove the point most people share similar pains and problems in common. We all individually have experienced directly, or been exposed to others who have experienced at least one of the fourteen (14) Life Issues. This is true regardless of culture, age, geography, education, or chosen field of employment. It is important to recognize as a Counselor that having difficulty working through personal issues in their own life can hinder ones ability to assist others with their recovery over life dilemmas and problems.

For example, if a Counselor has difficulty dealing with their own Grief and Loss of a family member, the Counselor may experience extreme difficulty allowing their clients to show anger or grief hence counter productive for the client's ability to work through their grief. The Counselor ultimately will block their clients from showing grief and anger in counseling sessions because their client will bring to light feelings uncomfortable for the Counselor to process. Therefore, the Counselor will "shut down" or redirect their client unknowingly when the Counselor begins to feel internally emotionally uncomfortable.

Overall what I learned from providing this exercise to both Counselors, Therapists, Graduate Students in training to become Psychologists, and Facilitators of Psychological Growth Retreats, is when exercise participates allowed themselves to be truthful of their unique experiences they rated the exercise successful and beneficial. In addition, that even Therapists and Psychologists have a difficult time telling their most intimate secrets of their life to complete strangers. As Psychologists, we by ethics, do not share personal details in the course of providing therapeutic services, yet awareness of the patient struggle is paramount to ensure we spend adequate time on building rapport. Knowing this may help those who provide therapeutic services to be more sensitive to others who seek help from them and struggle. Knowing this dynamics is *always* at play with a Therapist to Patient relationship in establishing rapport, will assist therapeutic Counselors in being more sensitive to those who do have a difficult time establishing trust and rapport with others. If you are a Counselor, Therapist, Psychologist, Psychiatrist, or in the extended helping profession, deal honestly with your clients and do not be afraid to allow patients to process difficult subjects. In moments of doubt, professionals should seek supervision, or other means of obtaining support for issues left unresolved for the professional. Perhaps obtaining individual therapy if warranted to work through unresolved issues if Professionals recognize their own personal issues begin to interfere with helping one's patients resolve important issues brought into therapy sessions.

The results of this exercise has application for non-professionals as well. What I discovered is that all individuals have difficulty self-disclosing and being *Known by Others*. My original study group of participants tested were Mental Health Therapists in Graduate School pursuing a Masters Degree in Psychology and they too experienced difficulty self disclosing in spite of their current level of professional training and possessing an understanding that truthful self disclosure is the core perquisite above establishing rapport to reaching beneficial change for their patients. The findings were not judged as either right or wrong but a reflection of the truth. A common innate characteristic exists towards hesitation we all share as humans when vulnerable, and it was noted as significant that most felt uncomfortable being assigned a *Life Issue* from the fourteen choices provided.

There are common issues we all intrinsically hold dear which prevent us from allowing others to know who we really are. The irony in this is that other people in general are so astute they probably know the dilemmas a person is struggling with even if another is attempting to mask their inner struggles. As hard as individuals struggle to conceal personal dilemmas, we also ironically use defenses to divert others. This calculated therapeutic *maneuvering* of sorts has always been the hidden mysterious arsenal of analytical talent professionals are highly trained to decipher through early with patients in the therapeutic process. Not to judge the dynamics at play, but as professional therapists foster a safe environment so the patient can feel comfortable enough to disclose the content they struggle with and process it within an empathetic forum, the therapist can provide better treatment.

Yet, people struggle to keep parts of them hidden from others. Consequently, for the person who works so hard to continue masking parts of themselves from others can cause the self undue levels of anxiety, fear, conflicts, sorrow, lost opportunities, and most importantly, delays in achieving Psychological Growth in the one area the person may have initiated a therapeutic treatment intervention to resolve. It hardly makes rational sense, but therein lies the irony and challenge most, even therapeutic professionals face, when helping patients.

Hierarchy Of Needs

Abraham Maslow, American Psychologist and practitioner of Humanistic Psychology, is known for developing a Hierarchy of Needs theory first proposed in a paper *A Theory of Human Motivation* (Maslow 1943). He later expanded his concepts to include his observations of man's innate curiosity. Maslow studied healthy people when most Psychologists studied those with chronic Mental Health disorders creating depilating symptoms and individual life unmanageability.

Maslow studied exemplary people to include Albert Einstein, Jane Addams, Eleanor Roosevelt, and Frederick Douglass, rather than the Mentally Ill or Neurotic Personalities, and explained that the study of stunted, immature, or unhealthy individuals can yield only a limited Psychology and a limited Philosophy. As discussed in chapter two, arguments presented in support of a shifting consciousness that is occurring influencing research projects to further our understanding of happiness is important as we go forward, and appear to be more in keeping with the intent of Maslow's body of work. This type of research focus is not only important to the professional field of Psychology, but to assist those in society become exposed to a broader scope of content Psychology has to offer.

The whole of Psychology may have initially applauded Maslow's core intentions to describe characteristics of healthy individuals in society, even igniting a passion in others to pursue Self Actualization, however the bulk of Maslow's work did little to impact significantly what would evolve over the years in the field of Modern Psychology with exception of a few researchers. And, even then their efforts are typically considered novel and unexpected.

It has only manifested in the last century that society as a whole became interested in literature addressing themes of happiness. It would appear those of late however, who have shifted their research efforts and are communicating to a larger audience their results of broader Psychological topics displays a new level of commitment in the field. Recent progressive researchers investigating emotional states of Joy, Happiness, and outcomes from Life Satisfaction Surveys as Psychologist Dr. Tal Ben-Shahar has documented in the literature influence recognition so widely anticipated towards the advancement of a Modern Psychology.

Ultimately Maslow's body of work speaks to a specific Psychology meant to educate individuals on achievement, concepts of motivation, and offers a knowledge base of published literature and Philosophy to life from which people can extract skills specific to becoming ones personal best. People are designed for greatness inherently and to become more one must surround themselves, study, and research, people who have achieved what it is they seek not the study of what is faulty.

> *Self Actualization is the intrinsic growth of what is already in the organism, or more accurately, of what the organism is.*

> *Abraham Maslow*

In his text *Motivation and Personality* (Maslow 1954), and *Toward a Psychology of Being* (Maslow 1962), Maslow argued that each person has a progressive hierarchy of needs that must be satisfied, ranging from basic physiological requirements, to experiencing a sense of belonging, or pursuing sexual intimacy, esteem, and, finally, Self Actualization. Self Actualization is the consistent striving towards mastery. This author has always considered it to be obtaining what one is capable of achieving. All in society are designed for greatness; all capable of experiencing all that Self Actualization encompasses, hence it is only a matter of applying oneself to achieve our own full potential. The question then becomes at what cost humans are wiling to sacrifice to become all that they are able to achieve.

Maslow (1954), believed that man has a natural drive toward healthiness as well as achieving a state of Self Actualization. He believed that man has basic biological and Psychological needs that must be fulfilled first, in order to be free enough to feel the desire for the higher levels of realization. He also believed that individuals have a natural unconscious and innate capacity to seek out its needs (Maslow 1968). In other words, man has an internal natural drive to become the best possible person they can be.

> *...he has within him a pressure toward unity of personality, toward spontaneous expressiveness, toward full individuality and identity, toward seeing the truth rather than being blind, toward being creative, toward being good, and a lot else. That is, the human being is so constructed that he presses toward what most people would call good values, toward serenity, kindness, courage, honesty, love, unselfishness, and goodness. (Maslow, 1968)*

Maslow's hierarchy of needs is often depicted as a pyramid consisting of five levels. The four lower levels are grouped together as deficiency needs associated with physiological needs, while the top level is titled growth needs associated with Psychological needs. While deficiency needs must be met, growth needs are continually shaping behavior.

The basic concept is that the higher needs in this hierarchy only come into focus once all the needs from the lower levels on the pyramid are satisfied. Once an individual has moved past a level, those needs will no longer be prioritized. However, if a lower set of needs is continually unmet for an extended period, the individual will temporarily devote more attention on those basic needs until they are satisfied, and then progress up to the next level. Our innate need for growth forces upward movement in the hierarchy unless basic needs remain unmet indefinitely. In Modern Psychology, we can technically refer to this as being stuck, or stagnant, but once an individual is made aware of one's basic deficiencies, most come to see the need to correct set backs and correct problematic areas of ones life.

Maslow stated individuals not only know what it needs to eat to maintain its health, but that individuals know intuitively their needs to become mentally healthy, happy human beings, and how to overcome minor set backs most find as their greatest obstacles in life, but are not entirely insurmountable.

This is not to say that only those who are conscious enough to pursue full lifestyles, it is the basic urging of all of the human species. Not selective for a few in society, but is available for all naturally thereby stating the possibility exist for all achieving a state of Self Actualization.

Maslow also regarded higher consciousness, esthetic and peak experiences, and the importance of moral and ethical behavior will lead *Man* naturally to discovering greater states of individual awareness to become more authentic people. When he referred to states of *being* he explained that the state of being without a system of values is Psychologically Pathological and that human beings actually require a framework of values, or a Philosophy of life to live by which helps people understand the world in which they reside. He termed it a cognitive need to understand.

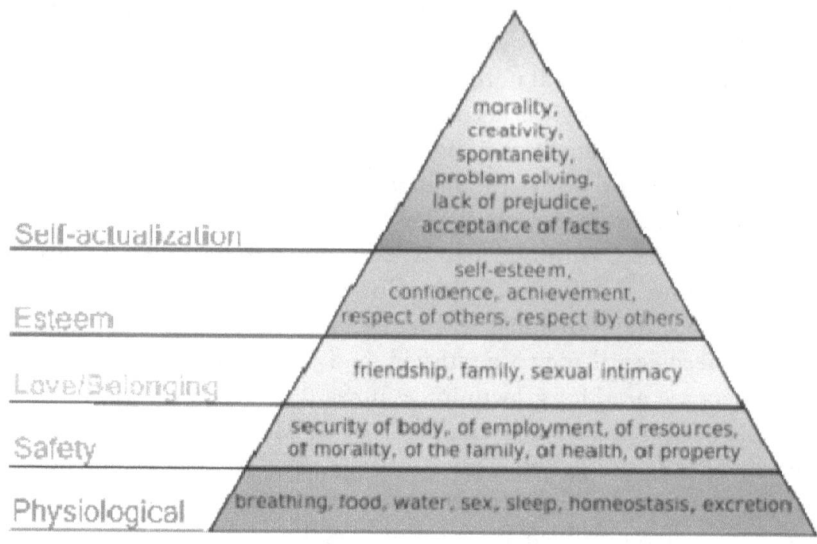

Abraham Maslow's hierarchy of needs represented as a pyramid with primitive needs listed at the bottom.

Maslow's Basic Principles

The principles listed here are the accumulative result of Maslow's twenty years of research studying individuals who were successful in expressing their full potential of talents, creativity, and achieving the top rung of Self Actualization.

The normal healthy personality is characterized by unity, integration, consistency, and coherence. Organization is the natural state, and disorganization is considered pathological.

Characteristics of Self Actualizing People

Realistic: Realistically oriented. Self Actualized people have a more efficient perception of reality. They are unthreatened or fear the unknown. They also possess a superior ability to apply reason to understand the truth. They are logical and efficient.

Acceptance: Self Actualized people accept themselves, others, and the natural world the way they are. They reject crippling guilt, shame, and enjoy themselves without regrets or the need for apology. They have no unnecessary inhibitions.

Spontaneity, Simplicity, Naturalness: Self Actualized people are spontaneous in their inner life, thoughts, impulses, and are unhampered by convention. Personal ethics are autonomous; they are individuals motivated towards continual growth.

Problem Centering: Self Actualized people focus on problems outside of themselves. They have a mission in life requiring a display of energy. Their mission is their reason for existence. They are serene, characterized by a lack of worry, and are devoted to duty.

Detachment: The Need for Privacy: Content with being alone and do not feel lonely when placed in this situation. They are unflappable; retain dignity amid confusion and personal misfortunes. They have an objective perspective. Considered self-starters, and are responsible for their own behavior.

Autonomy: Independent of Culture and Environment: Self Actualized people rely on inner self for satisfaction. Stable in the face of hard knocks, they are self contained, independent from love and respect.

Continued Freshness of Appreciation: Self Actualized people have a fresh rather than stereotyped appreciation of people and things. Appreciation of the basic good in life, moment to moment living is thrilling, transcending, and spiritual. They live the present moment to the fullest.

Peak Experiences: Self Actualized people have an ability to seek out and experience feelings of limitless horizons whereby feelings of ecstasy, wonder, and awe, can be experienced through ones efforts. A peak experience can be described as being in the moment where one losses their sense of time and space during periods of executing something extremely important and valuable.

Democratic Values and Attitudes: Self Actualized people are able to learn from anyone and are humble. A person is friendly with anyone regardless of class, education, political belief, or race. It is an all-inclusive attitude expressed to all in the human existence regardless of inherent differences.

Discrimination: Means and Ends, Good and Evil: Self Actualized people do not do wrong deeds. They enjoy the moment and process of getting to a goal not just the end result. Self Actualized people can make even the most tedious task enjoyable. They possess their own inner moral standards often appearing unscrupulous to others.

Philosophical Sense of Humor: The use of humor is spontaneous, intrinsic to the situation and is never used maliciously at the expense of others.

Creativity: Self Actualized people are creative in all areas of their life. They strive to be original, inventive, and less inhibited.

Imperfections: Self Actualized people are painfully aware of their own imperfections. They are joyfully aware of their own growth process and impatient with individual feelings of being stuck. They focus on real life pain, not imagined.

Values: Self Actualized people possess a Philosophical acceptance of the nature of his self, human nature, social life, nature, physical reality, and remains realistically human.

Resolution of Dichotomies: Self Actualized people's polar opposites merge into a third, higher phenomenon, as though the two have united; work becomes play, most childlike people are said to be most wise, opposite forces are no longer felt as a conflict. Desires are in excellent accord with reason.

Maslow's theory states there are two processes necessary for Self Actualization: Self Exploration and Action. The deeper the Self Exploration, the closer one comes to Self Actualization.

EIGHT WAYS TO SELF ACTUALIZE

1. Experience things fully, vividly, and selflessly. Throw yourself into the experiencing of something. Concentrate on it fully and let it totally absorb you.

2. Life is an ongoing process of choosing between safety over fear and need for a defense, and risk for the sake of progress and growth. Make the growth choice a dozen times a day that will include a significant amount of risk.

3. Let the self emerge. Try to shut out the external clues as to what you should think, feel, say, and so on, and let your experience enable you to say what you truly feel.

4. When in doubt, be honest. If you look into yourself and are honest, you will also take responsibility. Taking responsibility is Self Actualizing.

5. Listen to your own tastes. Be prepared to be unpopular.

6. Use your intelligence. Work to do well the things you want to do, no matter how insignificant they seem to be.

7. Make peak experiences more likely: get rid of illusions and false notions. Learn what you are good at and what your potentialities are not.

8. Find out who you are, what you are, what you like and do not like. What is good and what is bad for you. Question where you are going, what your life mission is. Opening yourself up to greater self awareness in this way means identifying defenses, and then finding the courage to give them up for the sake of achieving growth.

Fundamental Needs

We are born and exhaust our abilities going from one developmental stage to the next all along obtaining skills from which to build upon to make the next stage one we can master. Achieving the first fundamental basics in life is one of survival (e.g., breathing, food, water, sex, sleep, homeostasis, excretion through action).

Esteem needs come later where we master confidence, achievement, and respect for others and ourselves. Few strive for the later stage, but it is achievable.

Wherever you choose to set the bar that is where you land. It is also true that many set their bars for achievement extremely high, and then when the individual goals are reached, then become discontent, unfulfilled with their accomplishments. This is also normal because it happens in everyday life for millions. To avoid this dilemma one must be willing to consider repositioning their success bar at every developmental stage in life. You see the essence of fulfillment is not in the act of accomplishing more for the sake of more, or achievement, if we are unable to enjoy the process along the way. Fulfillment is found in the process of obtaining what you have predetermined as important to you the individual.

By contrast, if we idly allow *The Basics In Life* to dictate our life we become complacent with only mundane day to day living and this my friend is settling for whatever comes along, not directing ones life in the direction we would like it to be. True greatness and elevating above the basics takes decisiveness and risk. Some call it going to the next level. We hear this cliché in referring to anything and everything when someone would like to sell you something you have not yet achieved and they have the answer to *get you to the next level*. Rest assured I am not attempting to sell you anything, at least not yet, just encouraging you to be more aware now of how you are going about your life with what you have been handed in the present.

Are you settling or striving for excellence? Is there ever a personal choice to be made and you have chosen safety or meeting one's basic survival needs over a choice which would require risk outside your comfort level? Are you decisive about where you are now in your life, or allowing choices about the direction of your life to be decided for you without your input?

Subsistence Needs

Keep in mind there is one race no one loses. It is the human race towards finality. Everyone gets there sooner or later. Everyone will win at the game of life it is just a matter of time when the race ends, and how well one wishes to run the course. It is truly all up to you.

If I told you several years ago I had everything I needed would you believe me? Everything I needed to succeed in life to sustain me in a lifetime, would you be skeptical. Well it is true. I was born with an incredible capacity for greatness, intelligence, creativity, and compassion. Along the way I learned to be courageous, curious, adventurous, and appreciate the differences humans possess. You can get there too. My greatest accomplishments bar none to date is running with the bulls in Portugal, climbing Mt. Fuji in Japan to the summit, and receiving heartfelt love along the way in the most unexpected places. The ability to share the knowledge I have gained about Psychological Growth and Relationships through my studies in Japan, Hawaii, Italy, and California, in any venue I can deliver it, sustains me.

My preverbal bar in life is set pretty high. It is different from most. I have accomplished much in this short life and have much more to accomplish. I encourage you to continually question how you are contributing to the lives of others.

What are your greatest accomplishments in life thus far? Is there room for more?

Contribute or Risk Extinction

It is the law of continuation. Contribute or risk going extinct. Several people have questioned me about why my goals are not set higher, despite my accomplishments being uniquely above average of the statistical norms, yet they question as if in judgment. Why not more? I always reply that I have learned many years ago the greatest gift I have to give is to give my life away. My goal in life is to give to others in the manner in which I know best for me and I am not fearful of the results it will bring me. There is no certainty I can cling onto as I go forward and onward, yet I must go. If I can achieve the goal of contributing to the lives of others through a sharing of *what life lessons*

I have learned thus far, I will consider myself successful. Nothing short of this would give greater feelings of personal accomplishment and I only wish for others to have the experience of what its like to assist other's reach their full potential. It is a great feeling. It truly comes from an unconditional place of love. Moreover, to give this to those who may not have enough love for themselves is a lesson worth learning too. One's life is only as valuable to the extent that one is willing to give it away.

To live selfishly adds to the process of living. It is difficult to be lonely when you have so many people who appreciate what you provide for them. In return, others want to support you. Equally true it is nearly impossible to feel sad when you share a smile with another and they find within their heart an impulse to share what they have received back to you, or exert the same energy if not more, attempting to share the favor with another person. An audience who witnesses random exchanges of kindness are affected by just observing the act, then become likely to repeat this behavior in their encounters with random strangers on an unconscious level. Random acts of kindness are contagious for all those involved.

If we as humans are here for a short time, through history the only thing that remains after our death is our knowledge and the context in which we have chosen to share it. We can document our findings, have children, contribute to the manufacturing of a product, write history books, patent our technologies for future generations, establish laws for our successors to follow, dictate tax laws to ensure social engineering and foster future commerce gains. Every person will find for themselves a unique and creative way to contribute, not only for the life that will succeed you in death, but to create a creative legacy that will sustain the individual while they are alive simply by the day to day behaviors one chooses to participate in. Over time, this becomes the whole context of ones existence so choose wisely.

Adaptation

7f

To live passionately fully engaged with life requires adaptation. Being able to survive life with all its uniqueness, uncertainty, suffering, beauty, and remain creative and enthused about life requires a constant willingness to re-evaluate one's lessons learned along the way, and then make necessary shifts based on ones current level of understanding. Some would call it shameful to adapt to the extent we could engage in life as if we had no memory of the past. This would be considered an extreme attempt to run away from the realities in life that disturb us. Forget and move on. On the contrary, adaptation is absorbing what misfortunes occur, overcome them to achieve Psychological Growth, not in pretending devastating events have not affected us.

My reality is not the reality of yours and how can it be if we are each fully aware of how we live our individual separate lives, however there exist numerous commonalities at how we all arrive at finding new lessons for ourselves. To illustrate, in Los Angeles, California, I visited the Getty Museum, where I viewed the original work of the famous French Impressionist painter, Pierre Auguste Renoir. Renoir's painting *The Theater Box,* is of a couple at the opera sitting in a theater box. My first viewing I saw only the entertainment value of viewing how the painter so beautifully captured the moment of the spectators viewing an opera. At the time, I was also embarking on a self

---

7   *f* Pierre Auguste Renoir 1874 The Theatre Box. Royalty Free (RF) Photography.

generated indulgence to learn more about the French Revolution. Naturally, everything remotely relating to French culture caught my eye and attention.

It is difficult to find background information on *The Theater Box* by Renoir, but what I have leaned from my research at the Getty Museum is the male in the portrait enjoys the privilege of looking and admiring the feminine mystique, and the female takes great joy in being admired from a far. In Paris, it is apart of the culture to admire beautiful things, including people. The female proclivity is to be adored; it just comes naturally as all females are considered beautiful creatures, complicated, and possess a level of sensuality men are compelled to admire. It is truly the beauty of our innate differences of the sexes.

If you are female, appreciate your differences. There is no greater power on earth than the feminine mystique and men have the capacity to take you places you cannot reach on your own. And, men naturally are compelled to relish in the fancy of woman because by culture they are not afforded the same luxury. For the male, when in the company of a woman however they are afforded the fleeting opportunity to experience this unique level of self indulgent narcissism so intoxicating.

The second time I visited the Getty Museum, my perspective was vastly different. On the second viewing of Renoir's *The Theater Box,* my perception of the painting had shifted based on my pervious life experiences, the elapse of time, the adjustment to an unexpected divorce, then I could see all clearly from a vastly different vantage point all the complexity of relationships unfolded there in the painting. I could see then nothing more clearly than the irony of desire, which had eluded me previously, and the desirous lusts of wanting depicted in the painting by the couple, as well as the painting being a painful reminder when we individually contemplate consequences of wanting in *Adulthood.* I saw forms that then represented a memory of the dangers of seduction and of my own pursuits to satisfy very personal desires within the confines of a committed relationship. Viewing Renoir's *The Theater Box,* reminded me of my lessons learned to pursue my desires with more calculated intent. Perhaps I have learned what type of partner my feminine mystique has the greatest impact on, and what personal characteristics must be both appreciated and avoided at all costs so that I may experience love at its most deepest level as life intents it to be.

Progressive Growth and Consequences

Deficiency needs are Physiological needs enabling people to achieve homeostasis, crucial in keeping life in balance, which takes first precedence. They include the basics; the need to breathe, take in drinking water, to eat, dispose of bodily wastes, and the need for sexual activity. If these needs are not fulfilled, an individual's Physiological needs will take priority. Physiological needs do impact control over thoughts and behaviors, and can cause sickness, pain, and discomfort. When Physiological needs are met, Safety needs emerge. Safety needs include obtaining physical security of housing, safety from violence, delinquency, aggression, secure employment in order to maintain revenue and resources, moral and physiological security, family security, security of health, security of ones personal property against crime.

Love, belonging, achieving sexual intimacy, and meeting social needs, are found in the third level. It is the need for achieving a sense of emotional security in relationships such as obtaining and maintaining friendships, sexual intimacy with others, and having access to a supportive family structure. Love is the beginning of all wisdom, all sympathy, compassion, art, and all religions of the world. This author would go as far as to say *Love* is vital to all life forms and to express human *Love* to one another is what fuels societies. Human *Love* is the one indestructible thing in nature. This is crucial to ones well being and Mental Health for without expressing or receiving love and belonging, or meeting ones social needs, people may suffer periods of isolation, loneliness, Social Anxiety, or Depression.

Achieving these basic needs can be gained through the involvement in social organizations, professional organizations, clubs, sports involvement, mentors, confidents, involvement with family structures, or intimate partners both sexually or non sexual relationships. Without these types of involvements we see that people will attempt to meet this need even if it is in the form of negative relationships in order to feel apart of something intimate, or achieve a sense of belonging to gain another's support.

According to Maslow, esteem needs are on the fourth level on the hierarchy whereby individuals have a basic need to be respected, possess self respect, and to respect others. To achieve these needs individuals must exert effort to engage themselves with others or participate in activities in order to gain recognition from others, and to experience a sense of contributing to something greater than oneself.

Without these opportunities, a low self esteem may result in addition to feelings of inferiority, or an over inflated sense of self worth in defense of not feeling worthy. Not meeting these needs Maslow referred to it as developing an over inflated self importance or snobbishness. Achieving a high level of self esteem and confidence is so important not only for increasing ones likelihood of success in life, but it can also provide the motivation to initiate new projects, stay with projects longer if the person knows they can be successful if they just keep going. It shapes our character, our level of curiosity because without a healthy sense of confidence a person would be less likely to explore new activities in life.

Without self confidence a person may believe they will fail and never start. Doing so never really gives a person the opportunity to experience success, which is typically how people build their self esteem. Experiencing small successes along the way instills a sense of confidence that people can then use to tackle the next challenge. But, to never take risks is self defeating as it robs a person of valuable lessons to be gained by risking.

We all have value, but what will separate those who will pursue their dreams, desires, and passions over the long haul are those who have trust in their abilities to continue with the drive and commitment to see goals to fruition. Achieving goals takes risk, and courage, but in order to do either a person has to have faith in their ability that *if* they risk there will be some odds in their favor of being successful.

The Clutch Driver

Most people die before they are fully born. Creativeness means to be born before one dies.

Erich Fromm

What we have learned thus far is that Self Actualization states you must be what you can be. We have discussed the consequences of not living up to ones potential and conditions which may manifest if we falter in this progressive hierarchy of growth, but how does this striving towards Self Actualization play out in daily living. Under what conditions should we apply such a concept?

In today's changing climate of excellence, almost is not good enough. The physician who finishes last in his class is still referred to as Doctor in his professional circles. He will continue to gain the respect of others and will continue to receive the entire honor due him by his perceived accomplishments and rank in life regardless of competency level matched against his peers. This is how our society places value on categories and professional roles. The quality and dedication given to the physician's level of care extended to patients will surface eventually over time and there will be consequences to standards of care provided if competency levels are not maintained, as well as the damage patients can endure as a result of receiving substandard care.

It is possible to achieve significant accomplishments in life and still lead a life of mediocrity. Many do and are content with their lot in life, yet this is not the stuff that fulfills us. It is possible to achieve accomplishments in ones chosen field as a Lawyer, a Business Owner, a Manager, a Senator, a Physicist, or even a best selling author who gains recognition on the New York Times Best Selling List, and be mediocre in ones personal life, family or marital affairs.

How do we integrate the two? How can we ever be sure the choices we make will be worth it in the end of our short existence in this lifetime? The truth is that no one can ever tell us how. In the asking of how, what a person is really asking for is an instruction manual of what to avoid. They are seeking an easy template upon which they can mimic to remove feelings of uncertainty and limit fear.

Striving for excellence is important and can never be mastered until an individual is willing to recognize their own individual strengths and pursue those areas they thrive in. The strengths they possess to bring about the best in them as individuals. If a person becomes a specialist in their chosen field or a generalist, the question remains, is ones chosen field the domain they can excel in and feel most alive.

The danger we all face in settling for second best in any given profession, is a person will lose his innate creativity in the process to excel past barriers if one settles for less than their personal best.

The Philosopher, J. Krishnamurti, I have studied for the past seven years, through his many writings on *Total Freedom* (1996), explains people should never under any circumstance ask how to avoid becoming mediocre individuals because it takes away from ones ability to observe their own activities in life, their own thoughts, and their own way of life. When a person asks *how to*, what they desire is someone else to tell them what to do, some guide, some system, somebody to take them by the hand and guide them. The individual will lose their unique sense of freedom in the process. He further explains how these sorts of questions are better left for gaining instructions on concrete things such as how do I winterize a boat engine before the weather changes, or how to build a computer. Manifesting the wholeness of ones life is far more complex so Krishnamurti would recommend others to limit their reliance on another to gain this type of knowledge. It must be obtained through astute observations and in gaining self awareness.

> .....*to be Psychologically free and original can only come about when you are aware of your own inward activities, watch what you are thinking and never let one thought escape without observing the nature of it, the source of it. Observing, watching. One learns about oneself much more by watching than from books or from some Psychologist or complicated, clever, erudite scholar or professor. It is going to be very difficult, my friend. It can tear you in many directions. There are a great many so called temptations – biological, social – and you can be torn apart by the cruelty of society. Of course, you are going to have to stand alone but that can come about not through force, determination,*

or desire but when you begin to see the false things around you and in yourself: the emotions and hopes. When you begin to see that which is false, then there is the beginning of awareness, of intelligence. You have to be a light to yourself and it is one of the most difficult things in life.

J. Krishnamurti

In The Mist Of Greatness

Dr. Eric Berne many of us are familiar with because of his development of the Psychological theory Transactional Analysis, Ego States, and publishing efforts *Games People Play* (1964). Dr. Berne received a M.D., and then completed his Psychiatric residency at Yale University. Dr. Berne contributed to our current understanding of Psychology and dedicated a lifetime to his body of work. He worked to gain the status of Psychological Analyst and challenged Freudian concepts of the unconscious in his writings. When he began training in 1941 at the New York Psychoanalytic Institute, and later when he resumed his training at the San Francisco Psychoanalytic Institute, Dr. Berne obviously believed that becoming a Psychological Analyst was important. However, perhaps partly due to his aggressive challenging of Freud's widely respected body of work, Dr. Berne's membership application to become a recognized professional Psychological Analyst was declined. He was informed he was not ready, but perhaps after three or four more years of personal analysis and training he might reapply.

As told, the rejection was galvanizing, spurring him to intensify his long standing ambition to add something new to the field of Psychoanalysis. In the end, Dr. Berne suffered a massive heart attack while completing galleys of his new manuscript he was editing from the comfort of his hospital bed. Also in the end of his life's work, Dr. Berne searched for a mate, for love, the never ending pursuit of accomplishing intellectual recognition from peers, in contributing to new levels of intellectual thought in society, and to establish a balance between his life work and finding love, once all seemed within his grasp.

We all play Psychological theatrics with our lives. We hold so tightly either to a plan, or a goal, that we in the process forget the importance of finding balance in our lives even more so for those of us who have grand plans of changing the world somehow. There is a saying that Psychological Growth is not for the selfish because we must always give up something familiar, change significantly, be of service to others, and have a strong commitment to contribute. Notwithstanding, one will also run the risk of neglecting other important areas of ones life such as the struggle of finding balance, or maintaining important relationships in conjunction with other very important significant goals.

Think about it, this same dilemma is all around us. How many times have you heard the phrase *if I would have known this was going to happen to me I would have done things differently.* Even our brightest contributors to Psychology are not immune. The founder of The Five Stages of Grief is also known in the field of Psychology for contributing so greatly to the field of Psychological theory, and in the end of her life, she was met with great irony. Dr. Elisabeth Kübler-Ross, M.D., Swiss born Psychiatrist, introduced the Grief and Loss model in her 1969 book *On Death and Dying.* Her career was centered on the development of how counselors and professionals approach treatment for issues of grief, loss, tragedy, or traumatic experiences. The Stages of Grief include Denial. The initial stage: "It can't be happening." Anger : "How dare you do this to me?" Either referring to God, oneself, or anybody perceived, rightly or wrongly, as responsible for ones loss. Bargaining: "Just let me live to see my son graduate." Depression: "I'm so sad, why bother with anything" and finally, Acceptance: "I know that they will be in a better place" referring to the person or thing a person has lost.

Dr. Kübler-Ross' Stages of Grief and Loss applies to any individual significant personal change. One significant criticism of the Kübler-Ross Grief and Loss Stages is many in the field of Psychology believe lasting results occur after acceptance over ones loss ends. Without this one would be internally held hostage to the effects of regret and anger. The full effects of Grief Therapy commences really where the Kubler-Ross stages end after *Acceptance* and an individual gains the full impact of the reality of the situation presented. Dr. Kübler-Ross is reported to have suffered a series of strokes in 1995, then later died in 2004. A life which contributed so greatly to the lives of many reportedly Dr. Kübler-Ross felt anger and questioned her own legacy before dying in 2004.

The Cry of the Artist

A story first heard by Barbara Sher, a Counselor and author of unique perspectives on Self Improvement, tells the story of a young chef and artist living in Paris by the name of Babiet. It is a story of taking risks when a person discovers their true passion. As told by Barbara Sher, Babiet makes a decision to throw a fabulous party spending all her money. As with any decision made with impulsivity, a trusted friend is quick to intervene to convey unsolicited advice as well as provide a much needed voice of reason in the form of a call for Babiet to use restraint. Babiet's trusted friend questions "Why are you doing this?" Babiet responds, "I have been trained to be a chief." " Now you'll be poor!" her friend and confident tells her in a plea to convince Babiet to come to her senses.

To Babiet what she must do was clear. "I have been trained to be a chief. My dear I am an Artist. A creative person is never poor. I just want the chance to do my very best." This is the cry for all artists all over the world. You see right or wrong, it is an attitude many in our society have adopted. There are always consequences to all the choices we make in life and if not for those in our society who take risks, take the bull by the horns mentality as it were, much of the greatness we all benefit from would never materialize.

It is in the steps we take to come closer to what we desire and a willingness to take a chance when our conscious speaks to us after awareness. Results of our actions can never be measured from the beginning. This is not possible until the actions are taken. It is only after we have acted, we can then evaluate later how close our actions bring us to that which we desire most. Perhaps in the becoming of that which we desire most we manifest for ourselves a sense of renewed energy and passion, but if we only act on decisions we already know the outcome of as safe, yes, but this is not what will make us most fulfilled in the long run.

The manner in which we choose to live our lives is varied and unique as individuals are. Many of the choices we make along the way in life not only shape our accomplishments, but also through these accomplishments help widen our concept of what is possible. It has been my experience most have difficulty finding internal motivation. This whole process becomes less complicated if we first see the value, can see the possibilities and benefits to taking a risk to achieve what one truly desires.

This author is not advocating an all or nothing mindset for the reader to adopt, or making drastic life style changes for the sake of change. This would go against reason and often results in negative results if people are not responsible when approaching life decisions. To arrive at a basic realization that pursuing personal passions in ones lifetime to achieving true happiness and a sense of fulfillment is important. What to pursue, well that is what we all must do and determine for ourselves if we have the courage not to give into negative influences regardless of where they may come from.

CHAPTER FIVE

Psychological Growth Defined

*P*sychological Growth is when you learn to operate at a higher level of well being and adaptive functioning derived from self exploration. Psychological Growth occurs when an individual recognizes a need for growth, and then initiates opportunities for self reflection to gain a new perspective of self and others despite Psychological defenses which may surface. The important component is taking progressive action towards achieving significant advances in ones desired outcome, or established life plan. The process can be both initiated, and then paused, or it can be an elected slow process or rapid. The term Psychological Growth will be used vice Personal Growth as the author believes a more comprehensive Psychological component is missing from our current understanding in the literature regarding Personal Growth, along with the other associated term Personal Development which is often used interchangeably. Psychological Growth includes the advocating of increased personal responsibility; a *taking action* component as being an important step and that all significant growth can not be obtained without considering the nuances of mental processes that are engaged during the process.

Vulnerability

First, know up front there is troubling news in pursuing Psychological Growth. A person cannot grow without allowing others to know who they are. A certain level of vulnerability is required to achieve maximum results in this noble pursuit. This is a necessary prerequisite and difficult for most to allow others to know who they really are. The risk of exposure can be met with disapproval from others, or worst, a person may fear the possibility of rejection.

Differentiation as we will speak more of in our chapter on relationships, is the next level in acquiring the quintessential important separation between "We" and "I" and in relationships it is often referred to as the Deal Breakers. To explain, when we are youthful undoubtedly our only goal is to achieve maximum acceptance from others. In allowing others to know us completely, we always run the risk of exclusion. We instinctively dread any risk that will make us unpopular. We question if we value what our peer group values and what the consequence will be to veer too far from the more widely accepted opinions and values of our peers.

The inability to choose for ourselves inadvertently aligns us to the most popular opinions and other popular values de'jur, but in the long run, what we sacrifice is not being appreciated for who we are fully. When we sacrifice showing others who we really are we naturally exclude those who would otherwise be more appreciative of what we have to offer. In life if we compromise in any part of the process, we compromise our full potential for happiness and yes acceptance by those who will appreciate us for who we are.

Courage

Achieving Psychological Growth takes courage. The good news in making a conscious decision to implement new insights into daily living and making different choices, those based on a more confident stance continually proves to be most gratifying for individuals. Most report pursuing Psychological Growth as immensely satisfying for those who decide on the quest.

Psychological Growth is the integration of ones authentic self in all areas of their existence regardless of its consequences. People commonly display different personality types in different contexts. At work, at home, or in career settings we display a aspect of our personalities that present to others what we think are expected personality qualities, or we only display those personality qualities that will serve us best in order to be viewed in a positive light. When someone is referring to Psychological Growth this means an individual is pursuing a full and total transformation from deep within themselves and not just a temporary personality change for a specific occasion or context. In all encounters with the external world, we bring ourselves and aspects of self are at play. Finding one's own comfort level to navigate this despite periods of conflict, or mental stressors, can be risky for most.

More times than not the consequences of going against the grain is extremely beneficial and positive to the individual who chooses for themselves to live a life more authentically. Research has shown many fight to obscure certain aspects of themselves in the various roles they commit to, while others have discovered to be true to themselves is more meaningful and consistent with their chosen personal values. In short, to be truly authentic in all aspect of our lives, we must be courageous in the risk of being unpopular.

Consequently, as beneficial as Psychological Growth can be, many fear the weighty choices that must be made which prevent most from obtaining Psychological Growth for themselves. We may intentionally sabotage ourselves from that which will bring the greatest amount of personal fulfillment. For instance, a couple desires to take their relationship to the next level and one has difficulty relinquishing control, succumbing to vulnerability in the relationship to foster greater intimacy. In my experience, it is common to hear this dilemma "I mean I really like you a lot and would like to take our relationship to the next level," and then one gets nervous and attempts to find fault in their partner hoping it will create conflict, a diversion of sorts to alleviate internal stressors felt and end the relationship.

They question, "What does this mean?" To obtain something great, an individual must risk and in the process, a giving-up or subtracting something valuable to the individual in order to obtain in exchange something even greater in value. Often the exchange is beyond monetary value and cannot be measured other than it becomes invaluable. Yet with this considered, what it will take, few decide in advance it would be in their best interest. Or, we say we "want the good stuff," but fall short of taking the risks to obtain it. Either way it is a process so unique to the individual a Psychological Growth experience is better served as an investigational tentative experimental process.

Pursing Psychological Growth is a process to be experienced with ones partner. Maybe you have seen a similar dilemma. A couple has trouble in their marriage and resolve to seek professional advice from a Psychologist who specializes in Couples Therapy. Both are thoroughly frustrated with their current situation and have exhausted all conceivable options together to resolving the same arguments they have come to expect like routine. The two decide ending the marriage is not an option and elect to seek professional advice and consult of a Relationship Expert. They both decide in advance that they are equally committed to save the relationship. They both verbally express a high degree of willingness to accept all professional input and exert the effort needed to exercise a viable alternative to their stand still. Now, can you predict what happens next?

One partner spends weeks researching professionals. They ask for references from trusted friends and other couples who may have sought Couples Therapy, they research articles on the internet and seek out opportunities to share this information with their partner. They weigh out the advantages and disadvantages of going with one Psychologist over the next Psychologist. The two even narrow down their selection of Psychologists by the most narrow of selection criteria by location of office and what they believe will make them most comfortable in tackling their relationship dilemma. They decide on one Psychologist and make the appointment. In the first meeting with their chosen Psychologist, they lay everything on the table, and then brace themselves for feedback eagerly. After an extended pause, the Psychologist asks each to be the person they wish to attract regardless of anticipated disappointments. That evening the couple without discussion of the feedback provided by the professional commences a new search for a replacement Psychologist.

That which is needed is not always executed. This couple wanted help, but in reality, what they seek is an easy way out of their dilemma without executing the hard work, which will be required from each of them. In their mutual quest to find an easy solution to a complicated marital problem, miss the lesson they were meant to learn from their chosen Relationship Expert. In resolving conflicts, a certain amount of emotional confrontation and pain is involved in order to achieve growth in any personal relationship either with self or in a marital relationship. This part of pursuing Psychological Growth is never debatable.

People are predictable. A couple can imagine how beneficial the rewards will be in taking required actions to improve a relationship, but the thoughts associated with the feelings we anticipate that "may" surface in the process is often enough to call the whole thing off and revert to what is familiar regardless of how painful old patterns have become. For some, if what is required is prematurely viewed as too difficult a process in light of invaluable pay offs, most likely it is a question of courage to risk. To take personal risks in spite of not knowing the outcome is always preferable to achieve Psychological Growth, but not always practiced. Those who are willing to risk, often receive benefits beyond their greatest imagination.

If you have made it thus far, perhaps you have made a decision for yourself that achieving Psychological Growth at this stage in your life is important. Simply put, making the decision to improve your life is step one. The next steps require more effort on your part that will require courage, taking continued action, and a willingness to be introspective. The process in obtaining Psychological Growth we have found will deliver outstanding results when a person is willing to pursue gaining insight into ones life dilemmas, the ability to confront fears, risk the fear of rejection, the learning of new skills crucial in tolerating one's Anxiety, and their participation in a supportive community.

Psychological Growth Obstacles

The obstacles to achieving Psychological Growth is an unwillingness to self explore. It is in the anticipation of feeling fear that hinders a person's ability to show others who they are as well as harboring negative beliefs regarding concepts of change. A pessimistic attitude towards life perhaps fueled by past defeat and disappointment are main obstacles.

An unwillingness to self explore can be because some feel it is unnecessary. We say to ourselves I have no time to sit in a state of self reflection, or they tell themselves that it will not matter anyway. On the contrary, all life has an inevitable ending but it is what we choose to do while we are living that is the difference between a fulfilled life lived with purpose and passion, and a mediocre life that is willing to settle for less. Periods of self reflection helps us to ponder what is really important, and allows us to develop a calculated plan towards its achievement.

Many with a cynical view towards their ability to produce results may fuel an unenthusiastic approach to how they lead their life and hence creating additional obstacles to achievement. A cynical person may question *Why improve at all? We are born. We die. Everything else shares the same fate. Then why this struggle to improve? What is the use? Expectations can only lead to misery if we do not achieve. Why not just lead a life of no expectations and see what happens? After all in the end, it all ends the same.* The problem unfolding here is that life is meant to be expressed in a variety of ways. Not just once in an act of courageous acts, but ongoing to resolve conflicts with ourselves and others with the continual initiation of progressive actions towards achieving stages of improvement in all developmental stages of our lives.

We get stuck in our own need to avoid self exploration, allowing others to know us fully and difficult conversations that will lead to conflict, or a disagreement of opinion. Yet, all the while, those are the discussions we need to confront with confidence regardless of their ramifications. You may think tackling the difficult topics will further alienate another, or partner, but in retrospect, this is what is needed and takes great courage especially in cases where anxiety surfaces at the thought of even mentioning what a person is not doing, or you may have issue with, or what _you_ are not doing. It takes putting insecurities aside and entering into a discussion or situation with maturity regardless of its outcome.

Taking the higher ground considering maturity levels surface and regardless of outcome for those who strive to achieve Psychological Growth must continually question what they can tolerate individually. Maybe we desire more homeostasis with others, or we want to avoid conflict, and though it all, maturity will always be your best gage to addressing those situations, which need confronting regardless of the after math.

We learn from our experiences, and with every great achievement, there are opportunities to challenge ourselves in new ways over the course of our lifetime. A person wins a big race and is successful. He takes first place. After the excitement of winning the race of his dreams, he may question what to do next. What could possibly top the goal of his dreams? So naturally, he will go about setting new goals, even greater than the first, and accomplish success, then what?

Has anybody tried to live a life of no goal setting, no sense of competition, or mindset for continued improvement? Just going through life without expectations for themselves, or others? Many do, but I am a firm believer many do so because they are afraid of disappointment if they expect something will not materialize from their efforts put forth. A need to strive towards achievement esteem needs, and improvement are basic qualities of all in humanity. Even those who have been devastated by set backs, or have not lived up to their full potential, always wish for more. At least it has been my experience in treating individuals who have been devastated by their life circumstances comment, "This is not what I would have wished for myself," and if provided the support and resources to improve their seemingly hopeless situation, typically made a choice to implement necessary changes to grow personally.

Those who combat setbacks, which limit their Psychological Growth, are either unwilling, or fearful to confront unresolved issues they have been avoiding and this prevents ultimate growth. In my clinical experience, I hear this argument all the time. My response is often to ponder how the client is explaining their situation, and not to discount what hidden meaning there may be in their defensive stand towards the issues. For the stronger an argument is made by a patient against battling past difficult issues, the more likely it is this person should for their own desire to resolve an issue once and for all. What they require most is to give themselves permission to tackle the difficult situation they face.

When patients object, what they are really saying is "I don't want to relive the pain I felt when that occurred!" Patients struggle with the dilemma of convincing themselves that they are better now, and harbor misguided beliefs processing issues will make them feel worse. Besides, they say "I'm comfortable now. I want to stay this way....comfortable." The truth is if a patient is comfortable they would have no hesitation discussing any topic. It is only with topics which continue to give us pain, we so desperately attempt to mask or avoid.

As a Psychologist, I can empathize with this dilemma they face, but my initial professional stance remains true, in order to gain Psychological Growth and success over our life dilemmas is not by keeping things the same. It is only through the complete shake up does one grow mentally, consistently, emotionally, and pushing the boundaries of our relationship with self and others. The process of overcoming Psychological Growth obstacles does require awkward periods where one will naturally want to retreat and that is completely permissible. As rational, mature adults, ultimately we know what is best for us and people will make decisions they feel are in their best interest. As stated above the process of Psychological Growth can be either rapid or a slow process. Occasionally however people require a slight nudge to explore more, to go where they have never gone and in doing so will take them to a whole other level unimaginable from where they sit in the moment. As rational people, we must also acknowledge that we do not have all the right answers.

Personal Growth & Personal Development

The terms Personal Growth and Personal Development are interchangeable. Both comprise the development of the self as a whole. Personal Growth is most aligned with individual efforts to achieve success over individual life dilemmas, and Personal Development, living up to ones full potential, has become a new age leadership development training term to assist business professionals gain greater effectiveness in the marketplace. Often in professional business training, some treat the whole person instead of only focusing training on how a business person can improve on the bottom line to close sales. A professional business person brings to all his encounters in the marketplace a sense of themselves as does a parent in nurturing for their children. The terms Personal Growth, and Personal Development also refer to traditional concepts of Personal Transformation. These terms Personal Growth, and Personal Development are viewed as similar and interchangeable with Personal Development being more often associated as being a New Age term for Personal Growth.

For all extensive purposes, concepts of Personal Growth have a strong affiliation with Psychological Theories of Existentialism and Humanism. The Human Potential Movement originated from a social and intellectual milieu of the 1960s and was formed to promote concepts of extraordinary potential believed to be largely untapped in most people.

The belief is that if an individual put efforts towards exercising their full potential, others in society would benefit as well as the individual. The net effect of such actions would bring about a societal change where all would benefit in a positive way. The individual who adopted this belief and exhibit actions towards this common goal would experience in life happiness and fulfillment.

In modern Western American culture, Abraham Maslow, who authored theories of Self Actualization as discussed above, to date continues to be considered to have contributed the most comprehensive body of literature and theory to outline our current understanding of human potential. From his research, other theories originated to include the Human Potential Movement. Considered a Humanistic Approach to Psychology, both Abraham Maslow and Carl Rogers in their Humanistic theories asserted that people make rational, conscious decisions regarding their lives, and optimistically individuals tend to reach towards their greatest potential by a way of course, or a natural progress, innate in all of us.

Traditional Analytical Therapies

Because there are so many creditable recognized therapeutic options available for Professional Psychological Therapists to choose from when addressing dilemmas patients face in society, we must look at what tools are available now and are both most accessible and efficient. Early contributors who provided comprehensive Philosophies to viewing Psychological dynamics most in society faced included Existential and Gestalt Therapies. Fritz Perls formulated experimental therapies which stressed awareness and integration. Equally important was the development of Gestalt Psychology by German Psychologists Kurt Koffka, Wolfgang Köhler, and Max Wertheimer. Gestalt theory contended that the task of Psychology was to study human thought and behavior as a whole, rather than breaking it down into isolated instances of stimulus and response. Through Role Playing exercises, and productive Consultation sessions in which free and open communications are shared between the patient to the Therapist or Consultant, measurable progress could manifest. The "Grab Bag" technique, perfected by Fritz Perls, Gestalt methods, states one is free to use what ever works to accomplish the task at hand. It is proven individuals gain greater insight from a Role Playing experience that is more interactive for the person to solidify their understanding of a concept on a deeper resonate level compared to traditional talk therapy. There is validity to this approach as some counseling techniques will work most of the time, but not for all individuals.

A Therapist who practices this approach must learn to constantly alter course when counseling methods fail with a client. In addition, a good Therapist must continually perfect their trade through continued education and use methods which work best for the patient in any given situation presented. A great disadvantage of most traditional Psychological Theories presented in theory lectures and practice, are the rigidness in which therapy techniques are used to treat patients. Fundamental tools and techniques of Therapy must update themselves on an on-going basis and occasionally, replace old tools with ones which have more validity and produce results with those who seek Psychological Growth.

Sigmund Freud's Psychoanalytic Approach to Therapy is in a caliber all its own however impractical many believe in treating patients of a modern century hyper focused on speedy results. Many who have been followers of Dr. Freud have generated questions and developed insight using his therapeutic techniques and process in treatment and have moved on to apply improved versions of his traditional techniques.

Modern approaches to Therapy have proved to be quite effective. Theories explained by Dr. Freud, which remain fundamental to my treatment approach, are the development of personality over the first six (6) years of life. The stages are very important, but very strict. I believe we are shaped significantly by early stages of development, but it is a more gradual evolution overtime after the unconscious mind can be triggered by exposure to events that occur later in life, which can be in support of, or in defense to early meaningful events. Once a person becomes aware of the effects of not having basic needs met in early development, it is only in ones later years, does the neglectful consequences of gradual effects manifest into awareness as a problem.

One assumption as to why traditional Freudian Therapy has lost popularity over the years, despite a well known fact that most of his theories have been dispelled, is that not everyone has the luxury to stay in therapy for a year and never appear to reach a sense of accelerated Psychological Growth.

Traditional Freudian theories teach us the longer the exposure to the process of Psychological Analytical Therapy, the greater the results and through the analysis process with their Therapist may provide the patient with a greater sense of discovering who they are. This does not mean the individual sessions are longer, just that the patient has a longer period of time often extending to years in which to discover their self in treatment. Take the typical therapy session of roughly 50-minutes. The other ten minutes are for the Therapists to dictate notes or process billable hours for their services. It is this author's contention that traditional therapy may lose valuable momentum that is gained within traditional therapy sessions if a patient is not allowed enough time to process what they are "processing" in the moment. At one hour in a typical therapy session, professionals come closer to the precipice, closer to the core of patient's dilemma, and past comfortable defenses patients use to shield themselves. At one hour and 30-minutes we reach the core of the dilemma. While at the core of a patient's dilemma, which is half the battle for the skillful Therapist. The patient will make an important choice between continuing to confront their dilemma to resolution or can choose to terminate their depth of processing. Either way no matter how skillful the Therapist, the patient is ultimately in complete control of the speed in which they wish to achieve more growth. Caught in this quandary, the patient can easily deny, suppress, or disperse their issue onto something other than themselves.

There is nothing more satisfying as a Therapist than knowing "there is no escape" for the patient. Scary yes, but the process works. When patients are allowed more time in the moment they are:

1) Either force themselves to process difficult issues past their defenses that will allow then to grow.

2) Or, patients make a choice to torture themselves by delaying necessary hard work in therapy. They stop short of self confrontation. Patients give into and shut down after reaching threshold. With more patient-therapist trust, this can be overcome. It can also be referred to as the part of therapy that appears new; never explored before and the patient becomes aware that the therapy could go in any direction filled with uncertainty, which many equate with fear of the unknown.

This is the most painful pivotal point in the Therapy process, and is designed to cause the patient to confront their issue on a meaningful level. More than likely will also produce greater insights the patient can than translate into new learning then take action upon. It is at this point the patient ponders questions of "I should have" and "I wish I had the courage to" thereby the emotions of guilt and despair forms in the individual as the realization they are not taking action when the moment of self confrontation surfaces becomes increasingly more apparent.

Can people change their minds later after the window of opportunity passes in a Therapy session? Sure, but the character of a person and ego may get the best of them and they never do what is required if not confronted in the moment when inner Psychological conflicts surface through extended treatment sessions.

Sure many Therapists are advanced enough to manufacture this level of dynamics in a traditional 50-minute session you may be questioning, and it does occur. However, those with a desire to seek treatment with the overriding goal to obtain a level of Psychological Growth and progressive Development based on what I am advocating here, where therapeutic benefits appear to be more powerful, Therapy sessions may be beneficial if longer in length. Make the most impact, and meaningful to the patient, however remain rare in traditional Therapies. People require intensity in the moment to move past emotional and Psychological obstacles for lasting growth.

Let us take the example of the patient who enters Therapy for Depression. The concerns presented initially in treatment is the patient feels he is a disappointment to his family due to years of evidence he presents in the first meeting. The patient presents clear examples of how unstable employment patterns, failed relationships due to an inability to commit when difficulties surface, and the general feelings of fear and regret he feels surrounding what may or may not happen in his future relationships. He complains of the emptiness he feels in the present and how hopeless his prospects are for finding a partner that will take him as he is with all his perceived flaws.

In the second session which lasts as long as the first session 50-minutes, patient Mr. John Doe begins to speak of his past relationships when the Therapist inquires "How did your last relationship end?" The patient willingly speaks to his situation at the time and how his partner seemed to want more than he was able to provide. He calls it "moving to fast" and that his partner "wanted to plan for the future" he states. As the session reaches its 40-minute mark the Therapist associates a painful dynamics this patient has been bringing to all his relationships based on a history of self perceived failure. In the moment the patient has the opportunity to process further how being so afraid to experience pain, or explore new relationship dynamics regardless of his comfort level, has kept him from taking action. Keep in mind it is a well known fact in the field of Psychology, patients often present a well orchestrated attempt to *hold the meaningful dilemmas* to the last 10-minutes of the Therapy process. This is not to say patients do this intentionally, but it happens so often even when the patient is paying for solutions perhaps it is a defense mechanism unknowing to the patient.   It is neither intentional, right, nor wrong, but must be addressed tactfully in the Therapy process if the Therapist can gain any control over their patient's natural tendency to avoid problems they wish to address.

Patient Mr. Doe, you see has never allowed himself to experience emotional pain so he shuts down every situation that has the potential to end badly. He just avoids all situations that presents with even a hint of what he perceives as a challenge to his competency level and will do anything to avoid feeling like a failure. Yet in the process, all that he has been avoiding prematurely he later equates as a personal failure on his part. The truth is that he has never given himself an opportunity to know if in fact he can handle or cannot recover from such situations in life we all face.

Now, in traditional Therapy the Therapist, keeping with what they have been taught to maintain appropriate boundaries and establish consistency for their patients so they don't ask for more than a Therapist can provide which is more time. The Therapist will proceed along ending the session by summarizing what has occurred in the day's session, what dynamics were at play, validate the patient for making whatever greater insights they were able to make, and firmly tell the patient we will return to this important matter in our next session a week or month later when the schedule allows. The Therapist has in fact done a good session by the book and executed a process of quality Therapy in analyzing the critical dynamics at play and reframing issues for the patient to ponder so he has greater insight into his unique dynamics and the session ends. Meanwhile, the patient ends their session assured in the next session they will together continue to process where they left off. The patient leaves the office and makes the drive to his next destination, and later the patient continues to process intellectually what occurred in session.

This momentum gained in the session concerning the critical dilemmas is cut short. The intensity, the emotional state occurring in the session where all the visual, emotional, and physical cues for that dynamics are at its peak is ask to be put on hold until a later date. I say the moment is lost to make important connections for this person both emotionally and cognitively. When patient Mr. Doe returns to therapy to pick the session up again, the factor of time and ones natural tendency to guard themselves will have taken hold contaminating the environment which was present before. In the previous session when all three crucial ingredients were present; the visual cues, the feelings connected to his experiences, physical cues he was feeling and state of intellectual comfort he felt in the moment, will be lessoned in intensity, if but all lost to influence significant Psychological Growth and lasting change.

This is the matrix or convergence of all states acting at once that creates new neurological synaptic connections to foster new connections, new meanings, and ultimately increased Psychological Growth and heightened states of awareness to achieve clarity that fuels new actions. It is the moment new perceptions about their predicament can truly translate into creating lasting change in people. Psychological change is most efficient when all states are in sync to impact new meanings.

Timing is everything as the saying goes and when we maximize the time we have in the moment amazing things do happen. Can you imagine what would happen to patient Mr. Doe if he ended his session at the point of an important break through, and envision what would happen if you continued his Therapy for another thirty minutes in the trust of a compassionate and Analytical Therapist? Conversely, in life outside the Therapist's office, the same dynamics apply. It does not matter if you are patient Mr. Doe paying for Therapy to resolve a life problem, the Professional, or the average citizen, we are all subject to the moments which occur in life where we become forced to make a choice when important situations surface. The decision to stop short of experiencing a major break through, to make a professional decision to end a session when clearly extending would prove more beneficial, to pursue a goal and then stop prematurely despite ones conviction for the goal. Some call it being a clutch driver eluded to earlier. It is just what happens based on human nature and several very complicated life dynamics we are all subjected to.

What we gain from moments of true clarity, this is the moment we all make important new neurological connections, and we individually establish personal reasons to act or do something different. In the role of Therapist, if we are in a line of work that precludes longer sessions due to insurance standards, company standards, or personal financial shrewdness, then we make it an important part of the patient's written treatment plan to address the curst of things in the beginning of the third session. Alternatively, if we have the opportunity to provide services in a more extended format for example a Group Therapy format, we make sure we do not allow our patients to avoid processing fully important dilemmas in the upcoming sessions. The author is not advocating Psychologists violate ethical standards nor attempting to suggest Psychologist should establish inconsistent time limits for Therapy Sessions, only conveying that as a profession the traditional 45-minute hour "Therapy Process Format" seemly may not be the most efficient format for a modern time period based on what we know about human nature. This may be controversial because as Professional Psychologists, Counselors, Therapists, Life Coaches, and the like, we are institutionally instructed as a profession to *maintain limits*, other words like establishing appropriate time boundaries with patients, and also to be constructive with our time limits with patients is heavily enforced as a industry standard. This practice is also a savvy business practice consumers have accepted and have willingly complied with its enforcement. The practice of the 45-minute hour has quickly become a standard too yet ethically questionable when we view this evolving practice from the perspective of how the patient benefits from such practices. The only obstacle is that patients may not cognitively be on the same time line. It is our job as the professional to structure the session, as best we can, to ensure all patients benefit and the provider to be analytically sophisticated enough to verbalize to their patients the dynamic in the moment who may not share in the allotted time restrictions.

Never underestimate certain truths there are in life. Achieving one's passion is not in coming close, it is taking advantage of key opportunities. Moments achieved on the cusp of Self Actualization to know what you can become, and achieving it is an exacting matter of taking advantage of opportunity in the moment. Better served in the moment when opportunities present themselves. Not later. It is equivalent to the metaphor of the adventurer who goes into the woods unprepared and dies just sort of being only a mile from the interstate. It is the hiker who travels a great distance to climb Mount Everest with hopes of reaching the summit, and never makes it to the summit due to perceived unfavorable environmental conditions. For the adventurous climber who goes back to give it one more college try because the first attempt was not successful, on the second attempt chances are the same conditions will not be the same. The environmental weather conditions may be more favorable, yet there will surface another obstacle even more challenging than the weather posed. Perhaps one's hiking boots cause unbearable physical pain. Then what? On the second attempt, the players present that day will be different in all their unique personalities and level of mountaineering skills, level of enthusiasm for the goal at hand and ability to support their fellow climbers will be different. Take opportunities whenever possible as they are presented.

Encounter Groups

The efficacy of Encounter Group settings which allow for longer session lengths to process patient presenting problems can be determined by examining what benefits patients gain from their participation in such groups. To analyze critically whether a result of personal change is possible, the group process would be an important component to measure, matched against patient reports, and the effects of time. A thorough literature review on the topic found it fairly difficult to uncover clearly defined outcomes. What each individual receives from a Encounter Group experience varies from individual to individual. This may explain the difficulty in finding clearly documented results achievable based on patient participation at first glance.

An Encounter Group begins with interaction, according to Rogers (1971) and the group process. The purpose for an Encounter Group is to facilitate an opportunity for patients to experience a process rather than a product.

Encounter Group participants are afforded a rare opportunity to learn, and experiment with truthful behavior with others within the group process. Truthfulness is considered a fundamental basic component conducive to assisting patients meet personal needs appropriately. When a patient joins a Encounter Group experience they are believed to have hopes of receiving help from others in helping them to see how they make decisions according to Southard (1974). To be open to one's own experience is speculated to translate into one's level of openness to facilitating change within themselves. Encounter Groups such as those described by Oatley (1980), people can begin to experience themselves and others in ways, which are not necessarily familiar to people outside of the group setting. The individual comfort level patients feel in general, and how this translates onto patients sharing with other patients in such close proximity intimate topics of who they are in all areas of their life, affects overall individual expectations of receiving substantial positive outcomes of change.

The question of how to measure the changes effected through Encounter Groups is not a simple task as some will benefit, and some will not. A person who wants to grow in a helping relationship requires a good understanding of what the experience will entail and the individual has a high degree of motivation to achieve personal change in their lives. People who lack these qualities are better off pursuing other means of growth rather than in an Encounter Group experience states Verny (1974).

According to Lieberman, Yalom, and Miles (1973), the results of attending an Encounter Group are exhibited as the participants view them, or as viewed by others. According to four perspectives expressed by Yalom, benefits can be seen by the participants immediately after the group experience. Six months later, benefits can still be observed by the group leader, by friends, or relatives of the participant, and by other participants within the group. Yalom (1973) reported a summarization of Encounter Group member's perception of having experienced change. Participants' own view of change included those who completed the Encounter Groups. Approximately 50% to 70% indicated at the end of the group experience that some positive change had taken place. While not all Encounter Group members demonstrated obvious changes in behavior, nearly all members reported that they left the group experience with new positive feelings and insights. Members see themselves as more spontaneous, creative, joyful, and genuine. Group members have reported their lives as being less restricted by inhibitions, fears, and after the experience report having uncovered a variety of new found potentials, which can only be described as components found in Self Actualization.

Research proves that even worthwhile encounters do not produce uniformly positive and lasting changes in everyone. At the initial point when I decided to investigate what Encounter Groups give a person I had a few ideals of my own based on my past experiences as a Personal Growth Retreat facilitator. Through those experiences I discovered most participants generally reflect on personal issues that become the base for manifesting personal stressors, a lack of fulfillment, or anxiety in their lives. After the participant overcomes their fear of self disclosure to the group this paves the way for more inclusion into the group process of mutual sharing, both taking and receiving of unsolicited non judgmental support and validation from others.

From this vantage point, participants do achieve greater insight into their unique personal issues through receiving feedback from other participants from a fresh impartial perspective. In the process, the larger group members also become aware of what each participant wishes to avoid or not rid themselves of in the future after the group process. Participants are never given the opportunity to revert back to self defeating or negative thinking patterns while in the group setting because they are confronted by those who have grown to know their issues and what has been expressed by the participant that they wish to avoid. So, when the group recognizes inconsistencies from one another, these inconspicuous attempts to sabotage one self, are quickly addressed by the group members.

The Process

Achieving Psychological Growth at this stage in your life is important. Simply put, making the decision to improve your life is step one. The next steps require more effort on the individuals' part, which will require courage, taking continued action, and willingness to be introspective.

- Gaining Insight
- Confronting Fears
- Tolerating Anxiety
- A Supportive Community

The process in obtaining Psychological Growth we have found to deliver outstanding results in gaining insight into your life dilemmas, the ability to confront fears, learning skills crucial in tolerating your Anxiety. The most important piece is learning how _not_ to allow other's anxiety to become contagious. Gaining the support of others is an unexpected valuable gift most determine as indispensable to solidifying the learning process. The process of Psychological Growth in retrospect allows participants to reach greater confidence in trusting their ability to understand their unique patterns and merge this with ones thought process, which can fuel future behaviors, actions designed by the participant to obtain successfully what they desire most. Partly, this author believes is overcoming a once large stressor, the invisible barrier to growth, most do weather through. This process instills a confidence that ultimately translates into skills they can use to tackle other stressors in the years to come.

Personal change, which occurs in Encounter Groups, can be explained in two ways. First, individuals obtain an increased understanding of relationships and develop an increased need to establish significant personal relationships with others as a result of being a part of a positive Encounter Group. Secondly, participants uncover what is good and worthy within themselves so they can then move ahead to the future to seek creative change and innovation in their lives.

Therefore, while the Encounter Group is beneficial for some, and not for others, at least it sets the foundation for greater insight learning. The first encounter may not have dramatic, or long lasting benefits for everyone. For roughly 50% - 70% however, the group experience can be the beginning in the process of increasing levels of self fulfillment and achieving Self Actualization.

Overall, most Encounter Group members report they leave with a new sense of insight and positive feelings, and even a heightened level of understanding of their potential for establishing intimate relationships with others. Those who would benefit most from an Encounter Group experience are those who are suffering from adaptive problems, those who want to deepen their self awareness, the healthy free-spirited individuals who above all are not actively suffering from severe psychopathological problems or issues. Encounter Groups are not recommended for the Suicidal patient, or those who have been diagnosed with a Chronic Mental Health Illness in the Acute Phase, nor is it recommended for those experiencing crisis.

It is evident participant's attending an Encounter Group for the first time are hesitant. Many are shocked at meeting their future group companions, for the implication is that all are similar to them. All are admitting weaknesses and imperfections and are openly asking for the care and assistance of others. In addition, group members are concerned and confronted with the dilemma of wanting to maintain their individuality, yet wanting to change sufficiently to be accepted into the group by others.

The Growth Process: Slow And Rapid

Meaningful interactions take time and patience to develop in such a short time frame. According to Haas (1975), translating new levels of understanding into action is the focus towards the conclusion of the Encounter Group experience. The most fulfilling endeavor one can attempt is to pursue the goal of translating a new perspective, or new levels of understanding, into new behaviors. Obtaining new levels of understanding is an important step to take information and put it to good use. Talking about one's improved self is worthwhile, but the discovery of one's potential and the expression of emotions are far more valid when followed by a change in behavior. For instance, an Encounter Group member who has always viewed intimate interactions with others as problematic learns to initiate appropriate relationships with strangers. A participant who was once entirely domineering learns skills and strategies to practice greater flexibility in encounters with others; diligently listening to the needs and directions of others is viewed as positive change as a direct result of a Encounter Group experience.

In an Encounter Group or Psychological Growth experience, life experiences expressed vary from Phase of Life difficulties, Loss, Trauma, to ones individual quest for happiness, or a deep desire to help others.

In one example of overcoming divorce, the divorcee learns that all is not lost and they can pick up the pieces again instead of increasing states of isolation. They can process what has occurred, gain support from the group, and then develop a strategy to rebuild their life despite a change in their spouse's love and support.

Perhaps even change the story they tell themselves and learn to lose the story that says divorce is the worst thing that could ever happen. They become inspired for the first time in their life to make decisions that will direct their life in a new empowering direction they determine and direct. Take responsibility for the second half of life ahead of them vice grieving for what they perceive as gone. For someone who may attach their existence around their lost spouse, gaining a new identity based on self empowerment, fosters growth.

It is important to remember that not all Encounter Group members are encouraged to change their personality, job, location of residence, or marital status abruptly. Radical change especially, such as divorce or giving up a professional career, is usually not advised. Empowering change based on sound decisions that will bring out the best in an individual is recommended.

To illustrate, participant Ms. Jane Doe is unfulfilled and wants a change. Ms. Doe does not know what it is yet nor how to express it, but through the group experience and feedback from the group discovers a dilemma she has been struggling with for many years. She is confronted by the group experience and realizes why she has not had the courage to act on what she desires most. She has a passion for financial security and has little confidence in her ability to achieve it so she gives in to her fear and feelings of uncertainty instead of really going for it. Through the group she learns now that taking small strategic steps towards its attainment, the goal can become a reality in time. Great success she learns is nurtured over time. Therefore, with the support of the group Ms. Doe learns she will have to commit to implementing new skills necessary to hold onto her source of income, and part-time foster her passion that quickly turns into more than she could have ever imagined to support her and her family financially. For someone with an all or nothing attitude and misperception that life is only worthwhile if they can start at the finish line, are equally able to regain a reality based perception of what efforts, actions, hard work, and strategic planning can have in designing the life they desire. This "group think" experience of sorts, is powerful in that Ms. Doe may allow herself to be confronted by others who are able to decipher her Psychological defenses used; personal obstacles she presents, and provide her support and guidance to catapult her past the obstacles.

A beginning Encounter Group experience should not lead to drastic, irreversible life changes. What should emerge from an elementary growth group experience is a sense of new direction. For the novice, tentatively taking some first small actions is strongly recommended. According to Haas (1975), new ideas require nourishment and the input of another's more dispassionate assessment of reality such "group think" Encounter Group members can provide other participants. If someone is going to take on a new course of action then receiving feedback from group members first gives a person the opportunity to consider all possible options prior to implementing a new decision. Life changes under consideration, which involve ethical issues or humane changes that are thought out, should be relatively gradual. If successful, the changes are likely to be beneficial not only to the individual, but also to those with whom the person interacts with outside the support of the group experience.

It is not advisable to pursue changes, which involve irreversible, uncreative, or possible harmful ideas. Often in good encounters that have evolved cooperatively through the final growth stage, nearly all changes taking place are creative and worthwhile.

The initial entry into an Encounter Group is met with personal feelings of apprehension and uncertainty for most in search of self awareness. Participant's questions and inhibitions demonstrate their disorientation and alienation. Yet, invariably complete their self exploration process with new found potentials, and set out in new creative directions. Many actually reach a form of Self Actualization, others leave Encounter Groups knowing they have had a pleasant experience, but gaining little else. Those who leave disappointed may have been counting on receiving more from the group experience such as being "renewed" and there is no guarantee for obtaining self awareness or self actualization. For some people relations with spouse, family, friends, and employer are immeasurably improved, and their own abilities, talents, and goals are more visible and attainable than they ever thought possible.

After a Growth group experience terminates, participants seeking to ensure lasting results can increase their outcomes by attending post Growth group experiences weekly for four weeks to receive reinforcement of the positive experiences gained. These are commonly referred to as follow up Support Groups. The agenda can include opportunities to discuss new obstacles, which arise after the initial Encounter Group. As humans, when we learn something new, or make major life changes, new obstacles arise. If a shift is made in one area, an associated connected area is also affected. This is human nature to experience a learning curve in the beginning of learning something new, regardless of what the task is. When a group member makes a change it would be unrealistic to expect perfection out the gate. It has been this author's experience that with any new major change be it a pursuit for self improvement, or the anticipation of making career changes, new changes foster many new situations often it is difficult to anticipant all future challenges that may arise until the impact of implementation can be assessed.

In the beginning, there are only questions, and situations to look forward to that most have not even imagined. This can be a delightful time filled with all the ingredients for the adventurous and curious, or it can quickly become a time for panic if there is too much uncertainty and no set structure to voice obstacles presented. Feelings of uncertainty if allowed to impact judgment and ability to initiate new projects can interfere with personal efficiency and productivity over time. In follow up Support Groups which offer encouragement for participants as they embark on new ventures and how to incorporate new changes into existing relationships or life situations are highly recommended.

Another option, which should be an industry standard, is to ensure participants attend advanced groups and advanced Growth learning opportunities which will be more demanding on the participant to further intensify and engrain the new growth momentum. Those who had an initial growth experience and want to continue should limit themselves to groups clearly described as suitable for those who have already had beginning experiences and led by a trained professional. As a rule of thumb, it is advisable to limit the total number of encounter experiences after a second encounter to brief occasional sessions, or to have more prolonged and intensive experiences with ample time between encounters to allow the participant to measure their progress made. Encounter Group experiences that are generously spaced are more likely to produce rewarding effects over time.

Criticisms

Participants are confronted and encouraged to get disturbed by what life dynamics are no longer producing the results they really want. One ongoing criticism of Encounter Groups is that once participants are outside the group and confronted again by their personal limitations and perceptions of reality, participants seem to lose much of the positive momentum of their experiences gained while in the group setting. Many participants who are perceived to have been fully engaged in the group process, and took desirable steps while within their group, are always at risk of quickly shedding previous gains. Those who make progress in a beginning group should go on to groups that will reach deeper and be more demanding of them personally.

Outside of a group experience people are able to revert back to old habits, or worse seek out others familiar to them who will comfort them into not changing. If a group member is made to feel uncomfortable about settling in a negative situation, yet leaves the group convinced taking action will be difficult, they may seek out a trusted friend who may inadvertently pamper them into not making much needed changes. It's what friends do. We do not wish our friends to feel pain so we give them permission to feel better, right? Plus, if a friend changes, there is always the risk the other person will need to make change too. The group has no guard against this. This is neither right nor wrong it is merely human nature to seek comfort when faced with uncertainty. To undergo a significant change is threatening especially considering ones own level of uncertainty of the outcomes. We as humans find fear in the unknown as we can not predict how making Psychological Growth changes will affect us. Therefore, in the moment of uncertainty it is human nature to seek comfort from something known we can predict such as the comfort of an old friend to make oneself feel better. Although comforting, a friend who is not undergoing the same level of inner change may attempt to give their friend permission to stay the same.

This is not to say we have to find new friends but in any relationship, when one person changes it forces the relationship to change and this dynamics can be threatening. Especially in insecure relationships in which a partner may fear if the other changes too much it will jeopardize the relationship, or worse end the relationship if one partner does not in turn also undertake significant changes too. We will speak more to this relationship dynamics under the chapter on developing Differentiated Relationships.

Life Lessons For Psychological Growth

Is a Personal Growth experience for you? Well, why not ask yourself a few questions. What can you do now on your own to improve your life?

The biggest mistake many make is not learning from those who have already achieved the results they seek. Most, even in an age of global communication, still feel as though they must go it alone.

Do you like where you are and what you have become?

Have you ever wished that your life were different?

Can your relationships improve?

Are you producing the results you want?

What makes you feel good?

How do you reach the top rung and achieve success?

You wonder don't you? And, when you begin to ask yourself these sorts of questions you will look for what works. It is only then your journey to Psychological Growth will begin. Psychological Growth requires personal change that can only start from within with increased self awareness. The better you understand yourself the better you understand others. And, the more your relationships will flourish. Obtaining a self improvement plan for your Psychological Growth or Personal Development is paramount and this is how an Encounter Group experience, or Rapid Psychological Growth Seminar can assist.

Furthermore, it is highly recommended patients participate in both Professional and Personal Seminars & Training for their own fulfillment and Personal Development in life. The next step would be to take consistent and continuous action. You will do better if you work on yourself instead of worrying about your conditions that can fluctuate randomly often beyond one's control.

Ten Life Lessons on Growth

1. If you work on yourself, your life will change.

2. You have to develop your skills.

3. You have the choice to grow, to learn more, to become the person you aspire to be and mastering your life. For this part of your life there will be no supervision, unless you seek out help.

4. You can choose to stagnate, to hesitate, and remain fearful and doubtful and live in mediocrity.

5. You are responsible for your frustrations, indecisions, and lack of progress.

6. It is your choice. *It is always later in the day than we think*, and something new is not necessarily better. It takes courage to improve upon one self to make existing situations worth celebrating.

7. When you are clear on the direction you want to go and the lifestyle you want to have you will manage yourself and you will change.

8. When you change you grow. Know that the process of change will require a certain amount of pain and it *is a necessary step* in the process.

9. Mentors can assist you the best they can in helping you find the answers for yourself.

10. You decide what is useful. It is then up to the individual to choose what is valuable and important to pursue.

We can never really change someone; people must change themselves. But we can help. We can be a resource.

Stephen R. Covey

Psychological Growth Myths

In the quest for Psychological Growth one myth is that a person should seek it only when they are ready for the lessons it offers. In my training working with adolescents living in a court ordered Group Home placement center in Southern California, I was given the pleasure of assisting in their journey from court ordered mandates to becoming productive citizens. Based on their thoughts on Psychological Growth I learned few believed it was nothing a person should have to pay for. It was rather a frame of mind a person had to be in to absorb the lessons offered, and then apply them to their life. Psychological Growth was also viewed as something a person must seek out for it to have any lasting value.

With this in mind it became clear approaching the task of Psychological Growth would have to be in all respects accessible, informative, experimental, and practiced over time. Psychological Growth teachers do come in many forms and sometimes we never really know where the lessons will come from so it is wise to be flexible to new perspectives as those who require it most may not realize at the time pursuing Psychological Growth lessons have the potential to significantly change ones life in a more empowering direction. Psychological Growth is not a magical thing one sits through then is transformed. It is for everyone to pursue and enhances ones life.

Another myth to achieving Psychological Growth is that all seek it when in fact this could not be further from the truth. Not everyone believes they need to make any changes in order to be fulfilled or happy in their daily endeavors. Most are content in just existing with the basics. Neither blissfully fulfilled nor depressed in the depths of despair to fathom change would be helpful.

In my practice I have learned that "helping" is not always welcomed. Being a Psychologist is sometimes like being the keeper of special finely tuned tools and when offered, others are afraid to use them because they are unfamiliar with how they work, or afraid how they will be affected by the use of new tools. Wanting to help others compassionately and being met with skepticism I find is common. For the client it's like going to a busy train station in an unfamiliar location. The person initiates taking a novel rigorous ride to a new destination with only a promise the trip will be a positive experience and worth their efforts. What to expect next, past the pleasurable expectations remains unknown and is likely to generate anxiety and hesitation.

My favorite analogy to being a Psychologist is like being a good curious detective on an important case. You arrive at the crime scene and everything appears to be tidy. This is suspect because the previous crime scene on your last major case had an obvious outward appearance of utter chaos and it was clear a crisis was occurring, or an intervention was needed and quickly in order to deescalate the situation at hand. At this scene however the detective inquires what happen? The response he receives is "Nothing is wrong." How can I help? the detective probes further. "Everything is fine! I'm OK. I don't need any assistance, we will manage on our own!"

Like the Firefighter when they see fire in a burning building, they rush in to help. There are flames visible from the street and domestic animals have found refuge away from the disaster. When met with disapproval, or we don't need your help here "Everything is fine" the Firefighter comes back either drained from the struggle, confused, or emotionally exhausted. Take any scenario the Detective, the Firefighter; they all have this instinct to help when clearly help is what is needed in the moment and quickly. We see that offering to help often has the potential to impact change in others, yet people resist to be helped. It is called Psychological resistance. Why some are more affected by personal crisis is not the question. The true nature of what is transpiring is that we are all affected by personal crisis and depending on ones ability to recognize when to accept support or not is as unique to each individual as ones level of self care, personal interests, and passions.

What the research shows is that a person who helps another, or does a good deed experiences positive affects in the form of endorphins which link to emotional feelings of happiness. Moreover, those who witness a good deed also experiences positive effects in the form of endorphins. Helping can lead to spiritual fulfillment for the person that offers support as well as the person who just happens to be in proximity of an executed good deed.

Denial in all its bliss is a wonderful thing. With denial people will fight to prove you wrong and walk away never changing their mind, or even mindful that gaining support may be of some benefit to them when offered. I would only caution feeling defensive, depleted, despondent, cynical, or indifferent to entertaining a new perspective on a stressful situation might lead to the professional offering assistance experiencing more of those feelings in the future, or worse compassionate fatigue.

CHAPTER SIX

The Complexity Of Change

*H*ow we endure change and achieve Psychological Growth is to understand the universality of emotions. We all share the same feelings although we may internally perceive that others could not possibly understand, or know what we are going through.

As humans, we suffer unique losses at different stages of our lives. This is a universal truth. A predictable level of translation is had by all those who care to understand another's experience, and then compare it to their own. Across the globe we all share the same emotions. To a small degree, some have more traumas associated to the intensity of their experiences however there are common themes we all share.

Behind every great individual accomplishment that has ever occurred, behind any great contribution made by man kind, there is a back story of hardship. Think about it. Think of a time when you felt most alive. Or, think of your greatest achievement thus far. Along with this you may recall the moments just prior to achieving success in which there was great sacrifice on your part to achieve this success, or a fair amount of uncertainty. Most will agree who have risked achieving a level of success they have memories of their projects initially as being the hardest thing they ever had to do, but the results were victorious.

> *Don't be afraid to fail. Get out there and experiment and learn and fail and get a rate based on the experiences you have. Go for it and when you go for it, you'll learn what you're capable of, what the potential is, where the opportunities are, but you can't be afraid to fail because that's when you learn.*

> *Michael Dell, CEO and Founder of Dell Computer*

As humans we are the greatest story tellers of all time. Especially the stories we tell ourselves. We can be either our greatest supporter, or self defeating. Who wants to be the villain of their own story? When we refer to taking a realistic inventory of our current predicament and begin to question what must be overcome to achieve greater fulfillment, experience more moments of joy, and personal success, we must not dilute ourselves. It is best to be realistic. Fostering delusional thinking is ranked number one on my personal list of negative strategies that interfere most in achieving Psychological Growth and success. Winners never make the mistake of expecting life to be easy or unproblematic. However, by default we may unknowingly settle on a story we tell ourselves which gives us permission to avoid tackling difficult situations or taking action on a problem when action is most called for. We bargain which is a good procrastination ploy we play on ourselves to obtain more time. We may even choose not to contemplate difficult decisions, which would get us our longing, and attempt to lighten the situation with other creative delays. We choose not to decide beyond the problems we face. Or, not producing because we may feel stuck yet is as dangerous as harboring delusional thoughts. If there is a distorted perception associated with the hard work that lay ahead to accomplish success, we might go for the stability of a "sure thing" that ultimately kills passion and motivation.

Never make matters worse than what they are. Meaning viewing your particular situation for what it is, not worse, or no better than what it really is. Initially, some do find it hard to face reality, but in the long run preserving your mental well being will be better served looking at your current situation for what it is. Minimizing your situation keeps you from seeing your situation as it really is that consequently obscures one's ability to perceive it as "a negative situation" in need of attending to in a productive manner. If your situation is bad, admit it.

Often we find that if people are not ready to see reality as it as, more times than not they have allowed themselves to become comfortable with an unpleasant situation, making it even more tolerable to accept. If you view your situation for what it is you can find suitable solutions based on the facts, not on half truths and only the good lies we tell ourselves to make ourselves feel better. Again, if your situation is really bad -- Get disguised at the situation! It is OK to be uncomfortable with unpleasantness. When you allow yourself to feel and see your situation for what it is we get to a point where we can say, "I never want to feel this again" "Enough" or "Never Again!" It is only then, reaching a painful threshold, an individual can begin to solve negative situations they face and avoid them in the future.

What two (2) unpleasant situations come to mind now?

1. _____
   _____
   _____

2. _____
   _____
   _____

What solutions are there for the two (2) situations listed above?

1. Solution 1: _____
   _____
   _____

2. Solution 2: _____
   _____
   _____

Be realistic. Given your current situation is it realistic to have all your needs met? Given your access to resources at this particular time, is it realistic to be provided help with what frustrates you? If the answer is yes, and you have not received assistance, what are your recourses to resolving the situation? Do you have some control? Are you taking action over the things you do have control over, or just looking for excuses to be angry and frustrated? Remember, the Bull Fighter always finds a notable opponent! Always!

If you are in a dilemma and not taking progressive actions to challenge yourself, you are choosing to remain a victim of the story you have created. Feeling less fulfilled in life is a direct result of ones own doing leading to regret, punishing others for ones failure to act, negative attitudes, and a self promoted damaging mindset to put first things last.

Life's Craziest Beliefs

It is true we share many common beliefs and to judge them would be unproductive. But rather if we can begin to recognize which beliefs tend to produce less superior results for people we can work towards avoiding them in the future. Ask yourself now, which of these statements would you say are the most damaging beliefs.

1. The world is a scary place
2. I am only alive to please other people
3. I cannot change
4. Change is difficult
5. Relationships are painful

Believing the world is a scary place will foster a sense of dependency on others to achieve a sense of safety, escape from fearfulness, and leads ultimately to unhappiness due to feeling wounded or damaged from past events. Fear is the beginning of depilating anxiety. Fear is the response to a threat before it goes to the core of our personality, and than can translate into a fixed perspective later influencing our daily behavior as we go about interacting with the world and its inhabitants. If you can conquer your fears, you can alleviate unnecessary feelings of anxiety.

People are basically good and it is only if we have been exposed to individuals who may have negatively violated our trust, safety, or security, the result is harboring deeply ingrained unconscious beliefs that all people can not be trusted. We cannot control other's actions nor our early experiences when we were relying on more mature people to shield us from harm, but here we are all grown up, then what? We can choose to forgive, accept the flaws of another's insensitivity to ones vulnerability, and adopt negative beliefs about the world we contribute to, or continue to believe in a distorted universal view that all people are not to be relied on. It is my hope for you that you arrive at a place where you are no longer telling yourself a story of victimization and one of empowerment. Fearlessness and possess the ability to express personal empowerment.

Dependency only fosters helplessness if you believe you are only alive to please others. Imagine all the effort it takes to constantly consider other's priorities above your own. All the while your needs go unmet. This is a noble quality to have as it is the foundation that propels most to contribute and help others, but there should be a balance of healthy boundaries and the belief that your needs are as important compared to the next person. A give and take in relationships with others where your needs can be met too. People pleasers are a joy to be around because they possess this wonderful quality to anticipate another's need. The danger is that a person who believes they can only gain validation at the mercy of others by pleasing another above their own needs, is selling themselves short by looking to an outside source to make them feel good. People must grow themselves up and gain the confidence to do this for themselves to truly become mature adults who are independent, self assured with a high self esteem.

Western American culture dictates one's individual value is based on your level of value in the marketplace. Your market value is your valuation of yourself. Hence, as we age we can draw the conclusion that one's self-esteem is affected as our social value decreases. On the contrary, what has become a widely accepted assumption about the elderly is being revisited as millions of baby boomers have chosen to delay retirement and take on a second career well passed the age of 65 where in previous generations many believed retirement was expected. Today, more and more aging adults are retiring much later in life and continue to define their worth in society by the terms they set. This baby boomer generation it would seem has set their own values and beliefs about what it means to age in a modern American society and achieving more than the generation before, appears to be the popular agenda. Therefore, they are of value. They feel good about themselves, what they can contribute to society regardless of age, and this can be easily translated into influencing society to change its perspective of what holds ultimate value. Typically, in European cultures, maturity is valued because the aging generation holds vast knowledge and experience.

In life, it is wise not to expect others to be responsible for our individual happiness. When people exceed your expectations, be appreciative, and express gratitude swiftly as positive reinforcement fuels repeated behavior. It is harmful to have "should" or "always" in your vocabulary. What happens when you get disappointed? What is your typical way of responding when someone does not live up to your expectations? How do you respond? At this point in your life, would you be willing to entertain there are multiple ways of responding to disappointment?

So out of the five *Life's Craziest Beliefs* listed, we can challenge ourselves to pick just one. *I Cannot Change, Change Is Difficult, Relationships Are Painful*, represent perhaps a cluster of beliefs that foster internal feelings of *defeat*, hopelessness and shape one's world view of how many of us in society maneuver in everyday living. Due to the inherit nature of life being a complex endeavor for most, it is never just one, but a combination of a cluster of beliefs we foster as individuals that accumulatively manifest into a larger world view that will ultimately impact most one's future actions and behaviors. The decision to initiate, engage, or to not, is linked to one's world view. One's willingness to be emotionally vulnerable to another regardless of outcome and consequences, or not, is a choice based on how an individual perceives their needs shaped by a world view.

The most damaging belief is feeling hopelessness as it makes the rest of your life meaningless. It leads to despair, sadness, and Depression. Mental anguish is by far the most unproductive state to experience and efforts to restore meaning, productivity, expanding ones social supports to find a greater meaning outside oneself has proven helpful. What is lost in the process is free will. The freedom to go where the wind takes you mentality. To venture out into the world filled with amazing treasures, and adult dilemmas. To exercise free will is having 100% control over the choices you make for yourself. Everybody wants free will right? What comes to mind when you think of all the freedom you have had to make choices for yourself? What major decisions have you made for yourself?

That's right the major decisions that seem to happen so fast and manage to have the most negative impact on your life. What difficult decisions have you made that have had the most positive impact on your life? Or, maybe it has been your experience that some of your most major and difficult decisions that occurred for you were not made by you at all, but by the actions of others. You just happen to be impacted by someone else exercising their free will. Has that happen to you? If so, give an example in detail.

Now, when left to your best decision making skills what do you make out of your current situation?

_____

_____

_____

_____

Just as a side note; when I think of free will the topic of substance dependence comes to mind and how drugs impact our ability to make sound decisions for ourselves. Any good Substance Abuse Counselor would surely challenge his group members to make a chart of all the major life decisions made and than add if the consequences have been positive or negative for each decision listed. This chart is more for a visual display so the group members can see just how large a part drugs have dictated the direction of their lives and not free will, reason, nor sound decision-making abilities. Feedback on this exercise is mixed. Some group members comment it is helpful, some say it is too painful to look at losses, while others provide feedback that they just want to start looking for solutions to their current problems and not mule over decisions already made.

Why People Decide to Change

What is the first step a person would have to take to make change happen?

Are you disgusted with your current situation? Are you at a point where you have told yourself, ENOUGH! This must never happen again! Angry with yourself enough to say change is a _must_ and are willing to make the necessary major changes and adjustments to your day-to-day lifestyle to make it happen?

People always change when they reach their threshold for pain. A form of successive pain, or due to outside influences whereby someone else will make a decision that will consequently affect a forced change for the person avoiding change. The first situation where a person decides to make changes on their own based on experiencing some discomfort and pain has better odds for long term success although takes more internal drive to sustain desired changes. In the latter where someone else is providing the driving motivation, an external agent, the likelihood of achieving long term success is lower. Typically, we find that once results are achieved at the urging of another person, when the external motivator is removed from the equation, the individual will credit their successes obtained on the other person and not from their own doing.

This becomes increasingly more problematic for people to maintain what success they do achieve as they come to believe they cannot achieve the same level of results over time on their own. This is why a Consultant plays a crucial role in facilitating others to achieve the results they desire prompted by their own internal motivation to do so. A professional will never do the hard work for their clients, but they instead provide specific tools and allow the client to generate and sustain their momentum allowing ample opportunities for clients to gain maturity and confidence in their ability to recognize set backs as learning opportunities and provide guidance to clients to see where corrections are needed.

The Psychologist, or Therapist who believes in this approach to change will ensure their client learns how to motivate themselves. This is a valuable step as when clients are on their own they will instinctively know what to do to make corrections vice adopting a mindset a set back is a failure and quit whereby stifling any momentum they have already worked so hard to achieve under the Psychologists, Therapists, or Consultant's supervision.

Change Is Inevitable, Growth Is Optional

When inspiration does not come to me, I go halfway to meet it.

Sigmund Freud

As unique individuals, we can choose to look at the concept of change as a complex state better served avoided, but in reality change is something we all must attend to. If we do not continually re-evaluate our strategies to make progressive improvements in the daily choices to improve our current state of quality and excellence we can be easily replaced. We must evolve into something better, something more improved, then we had been in the past. We can convince ourselves that *changing* is for other people and elect to not consume ourselves with the difficulty it would entail to make necessary adjustments, yet this is only another mental ploy to avoid the inevitable.

We all contemplate making major life changes at one point in our life then it becomes a matter of how much it will cost us to work towards meaningful goals we set for ourselves. Without change, life can quickly become filled with a disproportion of mundane trivial tasks we must complete in order to stay afoot of day-to-day living. I ask you to question for yourself, which of the two situations would help produce feelings of hopelessness; *To settle in life for something ordinary.* Something pedestrian only because there appears to be a lack of wherewithal to really go for what a person desires most. Or, *Not identifying for self what is meaningful.* A high degree of willingness to learn something perhaps new and novel will be required to experience the lesson of expansion to sustain what a person my establish as *meaningful.*

The laws of physics teach us that with every action, there comes a reaction either equal to, or larger than the initial effort put forth. Be certain that in life there are no accidents and everything happens for a reason. If you have not had to think of why making changes in your life is a priority now, what comes to mind? If you are contemplating making changes, why now? Why now opposed to five years ago, or five years later in life? How will the changes you make today affect you in the present and in the future?

What are three major concerns you are conflicted over now regarding your life?

1._____
2. _____
3. _____

> *Modern man thinks he loses something -- time -- when he does not do things quickly; yet he does not know what to do with the time he gains -- except kill it.*
>
> *E. Fromm*

As you may already be uniquely well aware, time is the only one true constant in life. It is the only thing in life that continues to pass, twenty-four hours a day, seven days a week, regardless of what we choose to do with it. For most, they day dream of what they would do if they had more time, or ponder possibilities if they would have done this or that differently. Living in the moment is a skill. It takes gratitude. To be mindful of the past, but also 100% aware that day dreaming never changed anything. Successful people can teach us that change comes in the form of progressive actions. Consistent actions towards a goal, desire, or purpose.

Three Effective Strategies For Change

Lesson One: Time Is The One Constant In Life

Fortunately for you time is on your side. Just for today, be grateful. Regardless of how great or awful your situation is, it is what you have for that moment. Your worst day is someone else's dream. In all that you may have accomplished even on a bad day, is perhaps just a tenth of what the next person is working so hard to accomplish.

Lesson Two: Appreciate The Moment

Appreciation for the moment gives us increased awareness of our daily actions and how they impact our perception of the moment. It is neither good or bad just the reality of the moment and in this state, can you find a way past what is displeasing, painful, or uncomfortable. Focused and purposeful will allow for your best decision making abilities to guide you towards action.

Lesson Three: Overcome Resistance To Change

Have you ever noticed that when you think about changing your life, you feel resistant? Many people say that they not only feel resistant, but they actually do things to keep their lives familiar. They do things like start a diet and then eat a candy bar on the first day, or quit smoking and then sneak a puff. There are some things you can do to make yourself less resistant.

- *Eliminate Clutter:* Clutter can be viewed as a sign of uncertainty. Accumulating "stuff" might be stopping you from committing to an important situation. If you keep a lot of half-started projects around, it makes it difficult to zero in on what is most important.

- *Start Small:* Thinking of your overall goal can be overwhelming. So manage your resistance by choosing one small part of it and attacking it today. Let's say your goal is to lose 20 pounds. That can certainly seem like an impossible thing to accomplish. It will seem manageable if you tell yourself, "I'm going to lose five pounds by the end of next month and will maintain a scheduled routine weekly to track my progress."

- *Disprove Your Disempowering Beliefs*: In *Reinventing Your Life*, authors Young and Klosko, suggest identifying beliefs that keep you from succeeding. They offer a way to dispute those beliefs by asking, "Is there really any evidence today that this belief is true?" They suggest making a list of the evidence.

- *Remind Yourself Of Available Options*: You always have alternatives and the power to choose among them.

- *Take Responsibility For What You Want:* Look for signs that you are blaming your situation on others or not admitting past mistakes. Acknowledge them and move on.

- *Visualize The Future:* Author Barbara Sher suggests one way to do this is write an imaginary press release about yourself. The date is today's date, two years in the future. The press release is announcing the most extraordinary event you can think of. It does not matter whether this event seems only vaguely possible to you. The important thing is that it is exciting to imagine. In the process may trigger creativity to compile a viable plan to take action on.

CHAPTER SEVEN

The Elusive Concept Of Happiness

Happiness can be found in many forms. From the simplest of pleasures, to the most complex of situations. If we ponder too long in reflection we lose our momentum, if we analyze Philosophy we may become negatively influenced by the exposure to all the sadness and irony there is to be found in the world. However, if we live life fully, we come to an understanding of how best to find balance in life along with the importance of contributing to make life rewarding. We do not find happiness, we make happiness. We choose happiness. Self Actualization is a process of discovering who you are. Who you want to be and we individually pave our way to happiness by doing that which brings us the most meaning and contentment.

Life From The Side Lines

Life will never be satisfying sitting on the side lines wondering, analyzing, if it is the right time, questioning *If now is my turn to jump in the game?* Sometimes in life we must just go! If your asking the question if I could? You are ready to just take action. Of course you are ready. The question is will you?

Will you muster up the courage to live a life you design, one that is carefully sculptured to your liking not someone else's idea of what is best for you and you take it by default as if you had no input in the end result. We all have choices to make. The concept is simple, but few are really willing to make the difficult decisions that will ultimately result in success. Simply, there are two types of people when we talk on this subject. Either you take the lead on matters that will impact you the most, or you allow others to make the decisions for you leaving you with the result of someone else's best decision making abilities. Not making a choice or decision is not logical you see because in not making a decision, especially when a choice must be made, someone else will see the importance and urgency and ultimately guide you in a direction that may *not* be to your liking. Often, these end results are not to our liking but we settle, then complain later as if *everything was just out of my control.*

A few of the most popular questions people ask themselves as to why they can not take action now are listed below. When people ask themselves these questions what they are really asking is what obstacle can I use as an excuse for not taking action now.

1. What if I don't have the resources?
2. What if I don't have the financial means?
3. What if I don't have the proper connections? Know the key people to network?
4. What if I lack the necessary support?
5. What if I lack the know how or skills?

Too bad you will learn as you go.

The Learning Curve

Failure is not truly a failure. It is an opportunity for growth. It is a unique opportunity that should be approached with the perspective of being your opportunity to go through something you may need more experience with. To do things differently from the last time and improve your success rate.

Let us take the example of the partner who always loses their cool and any form of communication leads to a heated argument. This pattern of relating to one another has become problematic and if things do not change and quick, the relationship will surely end. The partner makes a decision to limit the arguing by practicing a new skill every time the same situation, or situations similar arise. Over time, he builds confidence with every situation that results in less arguing and more mutual understanding. In time, the partner masters the skill of effective communication, active listening, and persuasive debate skills to meet his needs, instead of fueling the process with increasing alienation with the object of his desire.

What Is Unhappiness?

If you are thinking about changing your life, you may be experiencing some combination of the following elements:

- Feeling Sad, Or Depressed
- Feeling Afraid, Feelings of Uncertainty
- Abusing Or Being Addicted To Alcohol Or Drugs
- Feeling Lonely
- Anxiety
- Problems With Relationships
- Not Getting What You Want In Life; Feeling Frustrated In Working Toward Objectives
- Ambivalence, Lethargic, Not Caring Enough To Have Goals

What Is Happiness?

If you are thinking about changing your life for the better, one way to start is by identifying your goals. You are probably hoping to find some version of happiness or emotional well-being that might look like any combination of the following:

- A Sense Of Freedom
- Increase Self Esteem

- Increase Self Confidence
- Be Happy To Get Up In The Morning
- Working Toward Goals
- A Sense Of Purpose In Life
- Satisfying Relationships

The problem with setting goals, in the traditional sense Psychologists have used them, is too rudimentary. We also need internal motivation in order to make our goals a reality. The field of Psychology it would seem has spent too much time on the directing of customers on how important establishing goals are, but have not spent enough time educating the public on strategies to develop internal motivation, which is the necessary link in connecting motivation to sustaining individual momentum towards achievement. We all want to think we can create our own internal motivation to achieve anything we desire, the difficulty is that we get caught up in distractions, self defeating patterns, or self doubt that subtract from our efforts.

When you decide to change your life and pursue happiness, maintaining a consistent level of internal motivation is key. Listed here are a few strategies to assist in the on going process.

Say Yes: Say yes more often to positive opportunities. Say yes to welcome others into your life. Say yes more often to opportunities that will allow you to experience more of life's vast wonders and complexities.

Explore Your Feelings: Keep a journal, talk to a trusted friend, and work with a professional Counselor or Psychological Consultant to explore personal feelings, which may be creating obstacles in achieving established plans.

Envision Your Future: Make a collage of your future with pictures or objects, do a guided visualization, talk to a friend or Counselor about your future, research the possibilities. Make a road map to your future.

Explore Wishes And Dreams: Explore options, make a wish list, and identify resources. Share ideas with others and request feedback.

Be Open To New Ideas: Take a class, travel, say yes to things you may have avoided in the past.

Look For Kindred Spirits: Avoid people who make you feel bad about yourself, seek out those who make you blossom, reach out to those with similar interests and dreams.

Try Something Different: Deliberately buy new items, try different brands, shop at different stores, do the opposite of what you usually do, see different movies, read different kinds of books and magazines.

Set Goals And Targets: Learn how to set useful goals, follow through, evaluate progress regularly, and reward yourself for achievement.

Take One Step At A Time: Divide your goals into tiny pieces and do one small new thing each day, starting now.

Look For Lessons: Remind yourself that experiences are not good or bad; they are simply lessons.

How To Lead An Extraordinary Life

There must be activity to have happiness or pleasure. Not the deliberate pursuit for happiness, but we achieve it inadvertently.

Joseph Campbell

The *call of the wild* is innate in all humans. This universal urge to explore limits, gain knowledge, or the desire to pursue new passions is normal for most humans. Exploring a new passion sparks desire, passion, a new found energy, and feelings of excitement. Where most hit the proverbial wall of defeat is when we pursue our passions for the wrong reason.

If we for example diligently pursue a goal for the sake of accumulating more, many find their results unsatisfying in the end. More is merely more and never equates to complete satisfaction in the end. So, after all the goals have been accomplished, many will begin to question *Why Am I dong this again?* Or, *What does this all mean?*

Why Do We Do The Things We Do?

So we get into the trap of settling for a safe position that will satisfy some need be it financial, need for approval or acceptance, or prestige, all along losing site of what the original goal was that sparked the passion in the first place.

At all cost, avoid what has been termed the *Paradise Syndrome*. The *Paradise Syndrome* is the name given to a relevantly new social condition, which gives the sufferer a sense of dissatisfaction, even though he may have achieved his ambitions or objectives, or fulfilled Maslow's Hierarchy of Needs. This term is also often associated with similar pop culture ailments such as *Leisure Sickness*, whereby stress prevents a person from enjoying his leisure time.

To combat this ailment, the following strategies have proven effective. The first is to be appreciative of other's unique gifts. It would be senseless to expect others to have the same level of skills and abilities we have, and we can learn from those who enter our life who possess talents uniquely different from our own. The second important strategy is to contribute. Contribute to another's Psychological Growth or Professional Development another may not be able to achieve without additional encouragement, sharing of wisdom, or the gift of another's time. Be Consistent. In life, there will always be better opportunities to veer from one's chosen career path, or to veer far from one's core beliefs giving access to more life wisdom, yet in the end consistency is what makes a great leader who holds steady the course to a core belief. Celebrate Your Successes. Find your passion. Have a purpose uniquely yours. Get out there and be active as a means to achieving ones own happiness and fulfillment.

PART III:

RELATIONSHIPS

CHAPTER EIGHT

Psychology of Relationships

The Romantic Pursuit

*I*f ask to think of your first automatic thought that comes to mind when the word relationship is presented, what comes to mind? Is the thought *No thank you, I have had some bad experiences*, or *Yes, I enjoy being in a relationship and I actively engage them in my life*. No matter what the initial reaction is, we have a starting point in which to explore more within this section on finding strategies to foster more enduring quality relationships.

No matter how well adjusted people consider themselves to be it is common for even our most *normal* in the population to experience negative visceral reactions on the topic of relationships. This is partly due to the inherent nature of relationships. Confounded by past negative emotional memories, subsequently impact significantly one's propensity to then displace, or even reenact conflict riddled relationship perceptions onto one's mate in the present. It is in the process of pursuing, engaging in relationships, and becoming more intimate with others that one's emotional memories can be brought to the forefront for most. With increasingly more engagement in intimate relationships, the full impact of this effect is seen clearly.

What typically occurs next, individuals will seek to avoid emotional pain by avoiding all relationships as an extreme choice, or will make a choice to settle for a less than satisfying relationship because it has less potential for conflict. Or, the level of emotional maturity required to pursue a quality relationship, may become viewed as too difficult.

Healthy quality relationships is the last true interpersonal marker we have in human nature to measure overall Psychological wellness. What gets in the way of loving deeply is ones perception of past pain felt stemming from another's emotional neglect, maltreatment, or past conflicts which remain unresolved. Matters of abuse, loss, feeling disappointment, or deep seeded past beliefs of inadequacies, all contribute to limiting one's overall ability to achieve Psychological wellness. Confronting those issues allows a person to love deeply past self-imposed defenses or ingrained negative belief systems.

In this chapter on relationships, we get clear. Marriage is not a love affair that lasts it is an ordeal. In committed intimate relationships with multiple layered benefits, albeit often difficult to navigate due to their inherit ability to trigger one's internal conflicts, remain worth pursing. The lustful antics we are willing to put forth in our initial efforts to obtain a suitable relationship are exciting and can be just enough to keep us off kilter. Maybe at first, but then when the elixir of lust fades, most couples are then confronted with the only question worth pondering which is to question if the person they are with at the moment is worth committing to after all the facades have faded away with the luxury of time and increasing familiarity.

Typically, we are only consumed with thoughts of ourselves and what we must accomplish in daily living, but a person in love becomes filled with thoughts of the loved one displaying increasing behaviors to possess the object of their desire. One's focus becomes external directed towards pleasing another vice a sole focus on tackling their own daily stressors. A person in love acts differently. They are emotional, and act in impulsive ways giving free will to their desires to possess another. A notable behavioral and emotional shift occurs which prompts increased decisive behavior to pursue their set target of desire victoriously. These are moments of Psychological surrender allowing our internal desires to be satisfied and consumed by novel pleasurable feelings. The pleasurable distraction takes us away from daily stressors and provides a powerful reminder of what is innocent and vulnerable in life; to be wanted, desired, and passionately pursued by another in a genuine way.

Initially, we are romantically intrigued with our partner and we find such pursuits to learn more about them stimulating. Even the simplest of interactions shared together become pleasurable events, and offer a window of opportunity to learn more about them, and of their intentions towards another romantically.

We are curious about what fuels their imagination and their interests. Innocent outings together to explore limits and boundaries about the other is the same pursuit millions have engaged in over the centuries. It is the basic romantic dance of the pursuit. The mutual sharing of simple pleasures such as sharing a conversation over café at your local coffee shop, or the sharing of innocent conversation with your partner, the nuances of why you like a new song you just discovered, all provide opportunities to connect with your partner in a unique and novel way. We analyze each moment as if it holds some hidden meaning, or will allow us special insight into our potential partner's most hidden infatuations for us as well as their most hidden desires.

Potential intimate partners who place more value in this phase of the romantic relationship pursuit, and extend more effort in their choices may be attempting to heighten the possibility in connecting to another's individual likes or personal interests. The potential partner who approaches these initial innocent stages of romantic pursuit should never go unnoticed, nor should be discarded to the side as a nice coincidence you just happen to enjoy. A magical occurrence in a developing relationship pursuit is a fantasy. Many experts in the field of Sex Therapy will agree that leaving things to chance is just an excuse for our laziness in relationships. Efforts extended early in any relationship can be considered as a good indication of the level of effort one will invest later when those same qualities will be needed to spark newness and excitement in the relationship later when greater relationship demands test our commitment, patience, or individual struggle to muster up one's strengths to work through tough times together.

Initial romantic pursuits are calculated and their purpose two fold. One, they allow the person being pursued a window into the level of effort a person is willing to extend for you. Those who do are giving and considered to be an ageless mature generous lover. Two, this is a person who does not approach love and romance lightly. Perhaps are sophisticated enough to know love and romance is not something to be taken lightly, but to be approached with the care and creatively of an artist, passionately.

Sophisticated lovers show signs of experience in the nuances of social interactions. The efforts they extend towards you may appear to be effortless and natural, however they are much more calculated in their efforts to make you happy. The sophisticated more mature potential partner is also aware not to violate personal boundaries too quickly. Confidence in character must be a strong suit to be successful in a romantic pursuit, and this personal attribute is viewed as immensely attractive to have in both males and females regardless of culture and time.

For example, a male pursuer may wish to explore another's sexual boundaries early yet will orchestrate this in a most subtle manner by taking their date to the cinema to view a movie with erotically charged content. The approach is slightly suspect, but the resulting after movie conversations discussing the content of the movie will have severed its purpose. Foreign movies offer an opportunity to become virtual travelers that has proven to have opportunistic possibilities for increasing familiarity. A date spent at the museum, or favorite art gallery with exhibits of respected artists, but subtly suggestive paintings and sculptures have the same effect. Furthermore, a romantic dinner date sharing family style servings can conjure up memories of family, or familiar themes of closeness with others whom you may have shared intimate moments with in the past that can be easily translated onto one's dinner partner.

In the art of the romantic pursuit, men over the years have developed an unjust negative stigma of going for the hard sell and can learn from what advantages surface from pursuing a soft sale to win over ones romantic interest. What we learn from history on this topic of gender differences is the female gender appears to be interested in the participation of engaged conversation, yet those of the male gender who are more inclined to be hurried, or seemingly more focused on getting to the point as it were, do not easily master this. When a male wishes to participate in, and initiates willingly opportunities that will satisfy most the fairer sex, perhaps appreciates its potential impact long-term. Taking the soft sale approach over ones gender dominate traits must be suppressed to be successful at romance or to connect and influence the female gender is perhaps a premature and limited view. What is required is willingness to incorporate activities to slow the seduction down; create opportunities to share verbally without the pressure of physical intercourse when pursuing the fairer sex.

To initially subdue a mate romantically occurs first Psychologically to have lasting affect and this assertion is true of both sexes. It may also be surprising to learn the sexual impulses of the male gender are key to this evolution of romance and can be incorporated into modern day efforts to pursue relationships that are more intimate.

The partner that takes you somewhere with limited exterior distractions, like those settings found in nature, on the water, or the seclusion of one's inner private scandium, bedroom, one's metaphorical den, does so intentionally for the similar benefits described above. Our histories greatest female reference to use this form of cleverness in romantic pursuits over a potential partner was Cleopatra. Woman of Cleopatra's era successful in obtaining power and influence learned to participate in *Psychological Warfare* due to their limited means available to them. To gain influence over Julius Caesar, Cleopatra invited him for a journey down the Nile where the two could indulge in sensual pleasures she created. The ambiance of the Nile was calm and relaxing in addition to offering limited exterior distractions other than those Cleopatra created.

During the period of Cleopatra's era woman had no real power. Women had limited social power and many were forced to resort to acts of seduction to gain any social status, or influence in which they lived. Power could only be accumulated through means of brute strength. Woman had only their power of creating Psychological influence. The lure of creating influence over another through means of lust was fleeting fore as soon as a male was satisfied, he could easily look elsewhere. Since then, society's efforts to employ the power of influence successfully as used during Cleopatra's era, can be found in areas of modern advertising, politics, even to argue ones influence in the court of law, all have their roots in earlier strategies of influence and the subtle tactics of seduction. These basic principles of seduction remain true notwithstanding time and evolution of Modern Day society.

This author speculates Cleopatra recognized even then that people are more inclined to feel more romantic when they are relaxed. Cleopatra's greatest ploys at romance were she allowed men access into a world that was foreign and uniquely different compared to the harshness of battle. She offered access, a brief glimpse into the feminine world full of self-indulgence similar to what we now believe to have greater scientific implications than ever conceived then. When a male is indulged either knowingly or unconsciously, in the indulgence of the feminine world, it registers memories subliminally to a phenomenon of significant pleasurable memories felt when the male was cared for by a female parental figure.

Modern day research connected to matters of love, memory and connection, teaches us there is a scientific Neurological connection to the Limbic System located in the brain. The Limbic System holds and carries neurological synaptic memories we store of love and feelings of connection. Those feelings we experience that are tied to earlier related memories of love register more and unconsciously trigger our perceptions as to whether *the person we are with* is either someone I am attracted to, or tells us if this is a feeling I am not familiar with. This helps us to formulate if this person is someone I am not attracted to. This pathway in the brain leading to the Limbic System is playable and easily manipulated if allowed to form repeated strong connections overtime. If a person is allowed opportunities to connect pleasurable feelings long enough to another, the greater the repeated connections, the more likely it is for an individual to manifest desirable feelings associated with the person facilitating those connections and pleasurable experiences. Because of this, we should never underestimate possibilities which present themselves as opportunities to instill repeated pleasant memories in the one being pursued in matters of love and romance.

Relationship Dilemmas

After the gratifying elixir of a romantic pursuit has long faded and all that which can be known about a partner is revealed, this is when the true test of relationships commence. Do not cheat yourself here. Do not sacrifice your sense of self, nor allow the occurrence of fading intimacy dishearten you. This is a normal part of _all_ intimate relationships. The heightened euphoric feelings associated with the process during the pursuit of falling in love are fleeting, and were never designed to last. Equally, do not allow this awareness to become a source of sadness for something greater, more intensity is possible if a person is willing to *continue*.

This is where the true work begins to build a better, more deeply intimate relationship with a partner, as well as the opportunity to grow oneself up into a mature adult capable of navigating any relationship dilemma.

It is important not to cheat at this phase of your overall accumulative Psychological Growth when engaged in an intimate relationship. Pursuing an adult quality relationship is often referred to as the last frontier to achieving Psychological Growth, and presents a unique opportunity to grow oneself up which fosters greater maturity. If we find ourselves in a quandary as to whether we need an intimate relationship, or attempt to make the argument it is just society's maladaptive attempt to convince its youth of today that relationships do not make us happy and *all* relationships must be avoided, may not see clearly the benefits. Research has shown even life expectancy rates are highly correlated with sustaining intimate relationships overtime. Research indicates for males, participation in sexual contact once weekly will extend their life expectancy rate by three years. For woman, it is the quality of the sexual activity they participate in and not the quantity that will extend female life expectancy rates in comparison with the male gender. Moreover, in research efforts to measure the benefits of one's level of perceived connectedness over social isolation, all show similar benefits conclusive in that one's effort to engage, and connect with others in a meaningful way, contributes to our basic human needs and contributes to extending ones life.

To often in life we find ourselves in conflict either with ourselves, others, or in our intimate relationships, that contributes to one's perspective on the benefits of sustaining a quality relationship. If the effort required to maintain a quality relationship is viewed as too demanding, or interferes with other life priorities, the natural tendency is to avoid relationships. This perspective on life is neither right or wrong. The author would rather like to caution those with this mindset to explore more and learn from others who have taken another stand on the discussion. It is completely within all reason to give oneself permission to forgo making a definitive conclusion on this one point until other arguments can be considered first.

In relationships regrettably when conflicts surface, immediately the focus can be on what someone else is not doing vice looking at what we the individual can change. In this section we will focus on what it means to take more responsibility in our relationships for our own happiness in life. We will also explore how important it is to engage in intimate relationships, as it is the last frontier for most to grow themselves up.

In a Differentiation Based Approach to relationships, the goal is to grow one self up and to allow others to be the people they want to be. The challenge most find in doing so is they become confronted with their own personal anxieties and personal lifelong issues they are either unwilling to address, or have decided the work required to overcome these conflicts are too difficult or too painful to endure. These feelings of anxiety then affect ones ability to confront important issues in their relationship, or worse, the anxiety can trigger avoidance in focusing on changing their behavior in relation to others because it is less anxiety provoking for them to avoid the issue all together. Anxiety is triggered by a discontinuity between what a person says and what they actually do.

For example, a female complains she wants more intimacy in the relationship but what she wants is for her partner to tell her she is okay to help calm her anxieties. In essence, she wants reassurance from her partner and may believe she cannot provide this for herself, which has negative consequences on so many levels. Relationships are uncertain. When you enter into any relationship chances are you will become affected by the relationship, even a changed person. It is a leap of faith. A giving up of whom you have been to become more, and there is no guarantee it will work out. In a new relationship, knowing whether or not it will work out is not a realistic expectation to have as it is an unknown entity that can only be revealed with time.

A popular band *Sugarland* has a song with lyrics *If you could just look in my eyes and tell me it will be alright, I just might believe* reminds me of the levels of neediness most, male or female, will find unattractive. Wanting another to reassure us in a new relationship does not bring out the best in an individual as it discounts one's own ability to be our best and display signs of confidence. When we seek reassurance from another instead of mustering up courage to reassure ourselves, what a person is really asking for is more commitment out of their relationship, yet may discount the level of their tendencies to seek excessive reassurance from others to feel confident or accepted. This is different. People will commit when their partner has the ability to love unconditionally and the other comes to believe their needs can only be satisfied by that person, not one's neediness to be reassured.

In a new relationship, this type of dynamics would be inappropriate because you may not have given yourself the benefit of time to evaluate if the other person is right for you. This is an important step to take as we *would not* want to settle for just anyone who displays so little interest in us. We deserve better. Typically in committed relationships where both have concluded the other can more than exceed their personal and relationship needs, verbal expressions of their commitment come naturally without prompting and behavioral displays of affection and intimacy in private and public appear effortless attributed to genuine feelings of attraction, and not obligation. Consequently, a forced premature demand for increased commitments in any relationship are not lasting and are to be avoided.

In another example, a male expresses a deep desire for more freedom in the relationship. He longs to be unleashed from the confines of an attached relationship in which he feels held captive under an intoxicating lure of femininity. Like the lone Cowboy however, when he gains his new freedom he wonders aimlessly. He does not know what to do with his new freedoms.

Only less differentiated individuals feel they *need* to escape. For the male, the solution is to take more opportunities to express his masculinity and tolerate the anxiety that surfaces from establishing those new boundaries in their relationship. It is anxiety provoking for both sides in a relationship to hear a partner say *I love you and I need more space*. These two statements are not compatible in any relationship. You can never have both needs met simultaneously given both components of needing more space, and generating more intimacy from one's partner at the same time. This is a unique dilemma in which the behavioral act of expressing a need to have more space will naturally create a emotional strain on the relationship hence the other partner involved will pull away emotionally to avoid feeling rejection having sensed an undesirable request.

To maintain intimacy at the same time verbalizing *I need space* is contradictory to the human emotional response in any gender. People are naturally attracted to those who invite them to come closer and exhibit a desire *to be known fully* without barriers of self imposed levels of personal defensiveness. Any intimate couple facing this common dilemma will reach its critical mass if this dilemma is not addressed head on by verbalizing individual concerns, and then responding with mature adult differentiated behavior.

Attraction and desire with polar gender opposites in ones expression of sexuality requires a necessary fueling of distinct passion at a level the other gender can understand and process. We conform to the other's gender dominate style to be accepted by them. Most, regardless of gender, trend to be attracted to those most like them. Concepts of mirroring, an appreciation of qualities considered feminine in females who appear to present a slightly masculine trait are viewed more attractive by the opposite sex. With this said, one would be hard pressed to say it is an all or nothing equation to developing sexual attraction. There are universal qualities each culture adapts as acceptable social norms in measuring the extent to which gender traits can be mimicked without appearing overly feminine or overly masculine to be excluded as being desirable to the opposite sex when they flirt with experimenting with opposite gender traits.

It is also a contradictory stance to take when attempting to establish those gender differences, which are so important to sustaining a passionate love affair over time. To make oneself attractive to the opposite sex, initially to gain trust; familiarity and desire, requires one to subtly mimic the qualities the other holds dear. And, once the desired affect is achieved, it will require a person to once again shift gears to re-establish subtly ones commitment to ones dominate gender position. Not an easy balance to juggle, but required over the natural progressive developmental laws of how relationships progress and reach an equilibrium for sustaining what they have sought to establish. Is it logical or understandable for the person who wants a conflict free relationship? No. And, that is exactly the point. The nuances of sustaining a relationship void of innate dilemmas must be addressed in order to be successful in order to achieve deep intimate levels in their existing relationship. The male gender especially will frequently find this increasingly difficult to navigate.

On the one hand, the male gender will tirelessly pursue an object of desire, even resort to tactics of seduction to win over their target, and over time may begin to feel perplexed by new urges for solitude. To balance their need to express male specific expressions of masculinity independently while wanting to avoid being perceived as if they *need an easy escape* from one's partner will require clear communication regarding the need for and enforcement of new boundaries.

Often times it is not that the male in this predicament feels an overriding need to escape completely, but an unrecognized need to redefine the importance of time for solitude and time spent with other men away from the primary partner. When a male spends too much time with a female partner, they adopt the partner's feminine patterns of touch and affection, consequently denying their male desires for more testosterone based forms of sexuality, according to David Deida, author of *The Way Of The Superior Man; A Spiritual Guide To Mastering The Challenges Of Woman, Work, And Sexual Desire*. Author Deida contends that when men spend an excessive amount of time with their partner, they can find themselves pecking their woman on the cheek, or giving her hugs and pats of "lovey-dovey" reassurance whereby the metaphorical female goddess and the metaphorical male warrior become neutralized householders sharing only the mildest play of sexual polarity. In this author's opinion, author Deida is accurate in stating there is an imbalance towards intimacy which occurs at the expense of a licentious sex life.

For those who have lost a sense of purpose, ultimately what is needed is austerity and challenges to realign ones masculine edge of power, or ability to recapture ones masculine direction. Once they have developed their full male potential without fear of it getting lost under the influence of the feminine wiles, a male will feel more joy in sharing their life with another.

A Differentiated Based Approach

According to author Dr. David Schnarch, who has published several books on the importance of differentiation in marriages to include *The Passionate Marriage* and *The Sexual Crucible*, contends that this approach of differentiation requires each person to face their own anxiety as a means to defining themselves while getting closer to their partner. Differentiation involves changing the way we think about our relationships. Instead of seeing it as the merging of two people into one, as has often been taught in both Couples Therapy and Sex Therapy, he contends we must learn to maintain a sense of ourselves as distinct from our partner in order to become closer to them. Gaining more differentiation is not easy Dr. Schnarch warns, but for those who choose to become more differentiated, the reward is one develops the strength to love deeply.

A Differentiated Based Approach Core Concepts

1. Have a clear sense of self
2. Develop skills to tolerate one's own anxiety
3. Do not allow partner's anxiety to become contagious
4. Display a willingness to tolerate pain for growth

There are four basic concepts necessary to sustain differentiated relationships. One, a person must have a clear sense of themselves. When placed under the influence of another be it male or female the individual can remain true to their unique desires, and maintain space needed to pursue one's individual and shared passions.

Secondly, develop skills to tolerate one's own anxiety. Tolerating anxiety in order to do the work one will need to do confidently as conflicts naturally surface in *all* relationships.   This requires people to shift away from a misconceived perception that they must always be safe in their relationships, and to display courage to stand up for themselves and be vulnerable. To develop skills for allowing oneself to be vulnerable in relationships is to allow ones partner to know them as they are; meaning we make opportunities to brazenly tackle difficulties that have lead to defensiveness despite one's level of personal comfortableness in confronting stressful conflicts. For instance, if a partner feels anxiety each time the topic of experimenting with sexuality in the relationship enters the conversation, instead of avoiding the conversation and further limiting possibilities, each partner should seek to allow the other to voice concerns. Communicate to their partner their fears regardless of ones perceived difficulty in maneuvering through a sensitive topic, or level of perceived personal intrusiveness. Then identify specific sources of anxiety.

Third, do not allow your partner's anxiety to be contagious, and lastly, display a willingness to tolerate pain for growth. One point we will continue to clarify is the misconception that in order to maintain a mature relationship, one partner must change something when flaws are pointed out by the other partner as being problematic. It is important for individuals to recognize their own behavior in relationships instead of fostering a perception that our mate is the one who must change to improve the relationship.

Regardless of what the other person chooses for them self, or what unmet needs remain unmet, we must always focus on becoming differentiated.

The Goal: Grow self up and allow others to be the people they want to be and only focus on what behavior you want to change in relation to others.

The questions this approach to relationships helps individuals answer is how to achieve more mature intimate relationships, and how to resolve unique life dilemmas which may have become problematic. Through a process of self confronting, and resisting the urge to become reactive, individuals learn to understand *how* their own unique life dilemmas help them to remain stagnant, hold on to what they do for good or negative gain, or avoid Psychological Growth in their relationships with both self and others.

Global Conflicts We All Have In Common

In my years of experience with Couples Therapy I have come to understand there are global conflicts we all have in common. And, future growth is impacted significantly if emotional dilemmas are not confronted by the individual. This is not just a matter of human ambivalence towards relationships that would cause an individual to avoid dilemmas they are in conflict with, or a self-imposed preference to deny oneself the pleasure of experiencing more fulfilling intimate relationships; it is a matter of courage.

When a person commits to addressing conflicts that will surface in their relationships, the anxiety experienced in the process is difficult and many become overwhelmed. A phrase taken from a previous Clinical Psychology professor, Dr. Susan Regas, Ph.D., this author believes sums up this phenomenon so beautifully. Dr. Regas explains it takes courage and a willingness to take *The Hit* to successfully accomplish differentiation as discussed in this section. Meaning an individual must exhibit personal courage to address their unique emotional life long dilemmas when they are challenged, including the anxiety that surfaces in the process in order to truly be successful in achieving differentiation in ones intimate relationships.

The process is the careful maneuvering through past emotional pain that surfaces when conflict manifests often triggered by the partner, and a person recognizes there is something they do not want to do, but must do to grow. In the mist of all desires to confront or avoid, can a person allow their partner to be the person they want to be, and stay connected to their partner in a way they have not before. The easy choice for many couples to make after they discover a flaw in the relationship is to just simply walk away. Find another satisfying conflict-free relationship. Explore another relationship that has the potential to conjure up all the pleasurable feelings once experienced in the relationship they want to avoid. The problem in doing so is you may be confronted with the same dilemma in your next relationship, and then the cycle commences again. Jumping from one relationship to the other all the while denying yourself the benefit of experiencing deep love that can only be obtained from self confronting; overcoming pain to achieve ultimate growth.

Doing something different in the relationship you are currently in may require facing the dilemma head on. Bringing out your best in times of conflict requires placing aside ones ego and overcoming the struggles of feeling accepted for who you are, feeling loved, the need to be taken seriously, or feeling an overwhelming need to be assured. Being enough, and placing another's happiness above ones own are the basic elements which allow individuals to bring out their personal best in times of extreme conflict with an intimate partner. If you can master this than you can consider yourself successful. It is a leap of faith many say because even after taking this step there is no guarantee one's efforts will be reciprocated. In moments of doubt a Relationship Expert can assist to navigate the intricacies of the dilemma. There is comfort in knowing that if a person chooses for themselves they must end a relationship due to irreconcilable differences, at least in ones next relationship, the person will be desirable to someone else who will appreciate the qualities this person can offer.

All relationships have conflict. This is one undeniable truth from which there is no escape. Combating relationship dilemmas are inherent in all relationships. They surface as a direct result of having to formulate difficult choices for oneself when disagreements surface in the relationship. It is this author's belief that the more we are able to establish committed relationships with others does provide opportunities for an individual to justly evolve; mature. Moreover, the conflicts which surface, while they will trigger areas in ones life they may have had difficulty confronting in the past can be addressed and resolved once and for all in the present so they no longer have to be obstacles in future intimate relationships.

The experimental process of an intimate relationship brings all those past issues to the surface allowing the person to process unmet needs. Be it past pain stemming from another's emotional neglect, abuse, loss, disappointment, or deep seeded past beliefs of inadequacies. Confronting those issues allows a person to love deeply past our natural defenses.

Confronting life dilemmas is part of the natural process of differentiation. So, what life dilemmas are you facing or avoiding? You can commence your Psychological Growth through identifying and addressing them or decide to leave everything the same. Taking more responsibility ultimately has more benefits and it is always more powerful when you don't give someone else the responsibility to reassure you, or feel as if you must designate someone else as being responsible for making you happy. Common dilemmas in relationships are the desire to avoid ambivalence with your partner after an affair, gain more trust with ones partner, avoid secrets, career conflicts, financial conflicts which trigger the perception of control over another. How to address a partner's addiction to internet pornography, parenting conflicts, the decision to provide full day to day care for ones parent, and the issue that is most difficult is whether or not to have children.

COMMON DILEMMAS IN RELATIONSHIPS

- The Desire To Initiate / Resisting An Affair
- Recovery From A Affair
- Avoiding Secrets
- Career Conflicts
- Financial Conflicts Which Trigger The Perception Of Control Over Another
- How To Address A Partner's Addiction To Internet Pornography
- Parenting Conflicts
- The Decision To Provide Full Day To Day Care For Ones Parent
- The Decision Whether or Not To Have Children

THE EMOTIONAL DILEMMAS

- Resisting Feelings of Ambivalence - The Deal Breaker
- Feelings of Trust
- Feeling Safe & Secure; Reassured of Commitment
- Open Disclosure; Displaying The Courage To Be Known By One's Partner
- Feelings of Anxiety
- Emotional Neglect
- Lack Of Ambition; Motivation
- Wanting; Wanting More
- Obsessions That Interfere With Closeness
- Triangulation
- Self Indulgence
- Lust
- Sexual Dissatisfaction From Partner
- The Abusive Intentional Need To Degrade Ones Partner To Feel Better About Oneself
- To Achieve Control And Power Over Another
- Sadistic Behavior
- Waning Feelings of Attachment, or Sexual Desire
- Violence In The Relationship

Two Choice Dilemmas

In a two choice dilemma, a person can not have it both ways. The topic of children conveys just how difficult it is for most couples to overcome and confront personal differences. If a couple has dated several years and all the while both holding decisively to the position they do not want children this couple is bound to make important decisions together surrounding their mutual agreements. One decision they may make together is to marry based on shared beliefs and visions for the direction their life will go together. They may hold a shared belief that not having children will afford them increased opportunities to travel and opportunities to advance equally in their individual career choices. Equally important is neither believes their joint financial situations will afford them the flexibility to reach shared goals with competing demands the added financial responsibilities having children inherently present.

After two years of marriage, one partner expresses a desire to have a child and the other does not, but then later *compromises* to the pressure from their partner out of fear of losing the relationship and avoiding conflicts. Meeting a partner half way through *compromises* does not work long term. The resulting decision to *compromise* is not an investment in the relationship, but a forced choice for one partner and may contribute to later regrets for the one who compromises. The negative consequences may be that the other does not give fully to the relationship, may withdrawal, and ultimately jeopardize the livelihood of the relationship lasting overtime because they regret their decision to *compromise*. It is far more powerful for a couple to process more the reasons as to why a change of plans is so important.

If one person's emotional need for greater intimacy is not being met by the partner in the relationship, and the addition of a child is seen as the cure to getting their unrecognized emotional needs met is problematic long term. Is the relationship at risk of dissolving and a child is seen as fostering greater commitment from the partner? Or, are their deeper issues warranting exploration?

In Couples Therapy we find that a couple who are so convinced they do not want children one partner may be harboring reservations that they do not know how to be a parent, or their childhood was marred with much pain. To be reminded of what was previously lacking can be perceived as too overwhelming to relive through the role of parent. The underlying issues are important to process because the end results of gaining greater individual insight will effect perhaps one or both of their ability to make different choices about the direction they choose to go in the relationship. Perhaps reach different conclusions based on emotional and intellectual insights that will cause them to want different things for themselves, and it is not a compromise, it is a personal choice they choose for themselves. Not forced. A choice initiated by the person has a deeper personal meaning and will result in a deeper level of commitment to sustain their decisions and quality of relationship in the future.

In Psychology, British Developmental Psychologist and Psychiatrist, John Bowlby's Attachment Theory is often referenced to explain the four types of relationship attachments formed in early development speculated to impact emotional developmental outcomes in adulthood. According to the Attachment Theory, since expanded by the research of Mary Ainsworth, and Colin Murray Parkes' contributions to explain its applicability to adult relationships, Secure Attachments are formed when a primary care giver provides a secure base from which a child can be assured their emotional and physical needs can be met. Parental responses are prompt and consistent which instills in the child confidence to transition away from the primary care giver and engage in other relationships. Most importantly, new relationships can be experienced with an ability to regulate their own stress and anxiety as it may surface.

Avoidant Attachments are formed when a child experiences from the primary care giver repeated unresponsiveness while in periods of duress. The care giver may discourage crying and prematurely overly encourage independence and exploration before a secure base is formed. A person's ability to express difficult emotional conflicts may become problematic later as an adult, and seek harmful outlets to express emotional feelings, or avoid and suppress feelings. How the process of Psychological conflicts manifests itself in a relationship with a low sex desire partner should not be confused as an avoidant person, but one who desires greater control over the relationship. The low desired male may appear reluctant to have sex with his female if he feels she is running the show. He may display behavior similar to being elusive and verbalize not wanting to engage in sexual activity, or when he does, he only participates half way. Many will discover with time this is an effort to gain greater control and manipulate the circumstances under which he will give of himself intimately with another in adult relationships.

In Ambivalent Attachments, the primary care giver may convey warmth and appropriate responses to the child, then later display inappropriate or neglectful responses in responding to a child's early primary emotional and physical needs. Later development is suspected to result in an inability to regulate life stressors appropriately. In adult relationships, feeling worthy of anything lasting may be in conflict with a mature relationship overtime or may feel reluctant to engage fully due to past disappointments. It is believed in the author's opinion the greatest obstacle to be overcome with this form of attachment style in adulthood is the person may expect to be neglected and not trust fully when presented with an opportunity to explore something more nurturing outside their comfort zone.

The forth type of attachment is forming a Disorganized Attachment whereby the child's early needs are met with parental intrusiveness, childhood maltreatment, parental withdrawal, or ineffective boundaries. An adult's later ability to regulate ones anxiety is gravely impacted. Additionally, skills necessary to regulate internal insecurities are also effected and do manifest themselves in later adult relationships with negative consequences.

All relationships have significance to ones overall development. Given that all relationships will encounter conflict, and a person will need to navigate anxiety that surfaces, does this mean that all is lost for those who fall into the later categories? No. We use our current relationships to grow ourselves up to surpass and move beyond earlier learned Psychological coping styles of dealing with life stressors in our adult attachments to others. Although the Attachment Theory is comprehensive, it negates the sum effect all experiences a child may encounter over periods of development leading to adulthood that can be positive and quite possibly prove to counteract any previous exposure to negative traits learned as a child. We can always give ourselves permission to learn and experience more appropriate ways of attaching positively, thus leading to an increased ability to tolerate our anxieties in relation to others. As mature adults capable and willing to self explore, we can also give ourselves permission to seek out nurturing relationships that are more apt to yield appropriate attachments.

As we have mentioned above, humans are not faulty at their core, we can only build upon that which we are to become more if we are willing to acknowledge conditions in need of greater insight, and possess the will to learn more. We, in essence choose how mature and differentiated we can become.

Can You Fix This Marriage?

The process of holding onto your sense of self in an intense emotional relationship is what develops your level of differentiation (Schnarch, 1997). Psychologists have traditionally looked for what is wrong with a couple who enters into Couples Therapy. The treatment as it were commences only after the presenting problem can be clearly identified, defined, and documented by the treating professional. This process, I suspect is important in the field as there is a perception made by Mental Health consumers the Psychologist is going to fix it. Many Psychologists, Couples Therapist, Marriage & Family Therapists, Counselors, and the like, believe they have achieved a sense of success if they can master this and ones professional competence can be drawn from resolving the problems consumers face. It can also be concluded what is occurring is there exist a level of comfort and certainty consumers achieve if assured the Psychologist can *fix* them, their partner, or the problems they endure. In actuality, nothing is broken. Taking the perspective of a non pathological approach to treating couples in conflict can make treating professionals more competent at their craft.

It is not pathological to have conflict. All relationships are expected to encounter conflict. Furthermore, developmentally the navigation through conflict is necessary to achieve growth. Experiencing conflict is not only expected, it is natural, healthy, and terribly suspect if couples never address conflicts, or fail to admit conflict exist. To grow oneself up in a relationship requires an understanding of how a partner naturally drives the other to grow whether they like it or not. One's feelings of love, if there is love in the relationship, will enable the partner to stay in the relationship long enough to see the other past their attachment dilemmas. Feelings of Love is what makes a person stick around when conflicts develop and helps lessen one's urge to abandon the relationship or worse make it disposable.

Whatever meaning there is in the relationship will have the greatest impact and holds the element, or commonly referred to as the important ingredient which helps each individual in the relationship to facilitate future growth together developmentally. Sure individuals can achieve Psychological Growth without being in an intimate relationship. They can seek out the help of a professional Psychological Consultant savvy in Sex Therapy, Couples Therapy, and relationship dynamics. Even seek the traditional forms of Psychological Therapy or mentoring from a trusted friend to resolve personal dilemmas we all face, but what unique dynamics that unfold within an intimate relationship is unmatched compared to a Professional Couple's Therapist or Psychologist, as these professions can only allow for structured limited boundaries. Intimate relationships trigger deep-seated issues like no other. Those relationship conflicts that surface can then be later processed in the Psychological Therapy process. If you are fortunate to find a therapist skilled in triggering those underlying dilemmas without the benefit of having an outside established connection, you are taking proactive steps towards achieving inclusive Psychological Growth. More than likely, those same issues confronted in the therapy process will surface once engaged in an intimate relationship where different anxieties and conflicts will be triggered.

Because of this, Psychologists must always be alert and suspect of patients who seemly grow more attached to the therapy process instead of investing those same energies into a relationship outside of the therapy session where it is not *safe*.

The process of undergoing Psychological Therapy is an intimate process whereby patients reveal their most intimate thoughts and concerns placing the patient in a position of vulnerability. All the while the Psychological Therapist is accepting, non judgmental, and offers a safe nurturing environment many report they have never experienced before in any relationship not even with those most trusted to provide those feelings. The caution is Psychological Therapist must be alert, consistent in their approach with patients, and provide role modeling of personal boundaries to best facilitate patients wanting to duplicate some form of what they like in therapy onto relationships outside of the therapy session.

Refusing to Grow in Relationships

If a person does not differentiate they will miss out on passion and an opportunity to grow. The ability to obtain and experience the full benefits of being in a mature intimate relationship with a partner may be lost if a person refuses to explore anxiety which is triggered by conflicts in a relationship. As human beings it is apart of our instinctive nature to want to grow; show progress towards some form of personal improvement. Also, as prevalent as it is for our human nature to possess this natural desire for growth, it is also natural for people not to choose stagnation.

Conflicts surface when we view our situation as being limited by choices to overcome stagnation. In fact, our society rewards efforts taken towards reaching ones full human potential through committed relationships, significant accomplishments, athletics, and many experience negative consequences for not contributing to society in a positive way. Without growth there is only one alternative and that is to become extinct. If we choose the latter, or someone chooses for us, it may lead to a host of negative coping patterns to include learned helplessness and dependency ultimately lowering ones quality of life if allowed to continue.

In treatment, a question I always enjoy asking patients who appear to resist choosing Psychological Growth over an intentional period of stagnation is "Can you see any way to improve your current situation?" as a way of addressing any resistance. This line of questioning is also helpful for those who present with resistance towards engaging in relationships. To take a break from relationships is perfectly permissible, even the length of time one chooses to do this for themselves is equally permissible, however for the individual who responds "I will never again have a relationship" speaks to an irrational conclusion they have reached based on a past of experiencing pain. Once more, what this person needs most is the courage to enter into a new relationship more mature than their previous relationship taking with them lessons learned on how to address and overcome their sense of disappointment. Not getting what we want in life can also mean that we have not clearly defined for ourselves what we value in life, or what we value most in our relationships. Defining individual values allows for a swifter disregard for those people, or situations, that are not aligned with our preset criteria.

With maturity, we learn not to deny ourselves of life's pleasure simply because there is difficulty, but we strive to make sense of the matter, learn from it, and practice new ways of being in our next relationship, or we may choose to grow ourselves up and improve the existing relationship functioning from a more differentiated foundation.

Quality Relationships

> *You can't lead anyone else further than you have gone yourself.*
>
> Gene Mauch

Relationships can be the source of incredible bliss, or a source of undying pain. They are the catalyst by which we can achieve Psychological Growth, experience deep levels of intimacy, and are our last real opportunity to grow ourselves up emotionally. This is especially true when in a committed relationship as in marriage, a common law vow, or a long term bond with a partner not dictated by a legal court mandate. In this section we will explore relationship barriers, deepen our understanding of the nuances in relationships, what qualities make up mature healthy relationships, and strategies to improve our relationships.

Quality relationships do not just happen by chance, they are cultured and natured. The old adage of what we hear from our elders is true; in order to have a good relationship takes hard work. I would go one step further and state that not only must couples do the hard work in order to obtain the benefits of a good relationship, but also to continue those creative romantic pursuits they put in initially long after the relationship has established itself as worthy of their individual investment to manifest a great committed relationship.

This is no surprise and the best relationships I have been exposed to have one quality in common. This is the ability to relinquish a part of their sense of security for the sake of the betterment of the relationship. It can be explained as a calculated intent whereby an individual decides in advance to behave differently, and make decisions which are in the best interest of their relationship without losing their unique sense of individuality. Not by resorting to the manipulative ploys so common with those who seek sadistic revenge with their partners to satisfy some unmet emotional need, but for the calculated who truly desire a deeper connection built on a foundation of unconditional love and mutual respect.

I have seen both through my research in studying to become a Couples Therapist and in my own life experiences, the process of finding a mate is made up of a series of events not entirely of your choosing, and can be based on glimpses of reenactments exposed to in one's past. To be the bride was my fantasy. Not the commercial depiction seen in the block buster movies where you see the scene of the woman destined to become the brides maid over and over again in the movies. Her depressing desperation to find a loving mate, the perfect one, yet only to be cast aside for the more attractive suitor who falls madly in love with her girlfriend. No. What I am describing is of a longing for something that is heart felt and not entirely of our choosing. Affairs of the heart are fickle and fleeting if not nurtured and maintained. We may have a template of what we desire most, but often times we are surprised.

My first lesson of this occurred at my mother's funeral reception. I was already in the mist of the developmental thirties dilemma of having already entered into a loving marriage and was convinced I had a handle on what marital bliss was. All the while, I continued to question what marriage was supposed to be, and I found myself longing for more insight, more answers, more examples of what this "marital bliss" is supposed to be so I could assure myself the experiences I was having were the genuine representation of our industry standard for couples. This was the first mistake. I was reminded of a lesson that day I will never forget. Looking back on what I observed, perhaps unconsciously, it was a familiar scenario I had been privy to for many years over the course of my lifetime I really had not given much notice to but had inadvertently always been the marker of reference for me of what a quality relationship was. This day however the lesson had more meaning as I was in a place in my life where the lesson had more applicability to my own current life dilemma. It haunted me more in a sense of what qualities a male would have to possess continually to express appreciation for their mate, long after all the disguise of knowing someone fully had all but dissolved with increased familiarly.

At the funeral reception I felt most comfortable talking with my uncle. I left his side briefly to go inside to welcome newly arriving guests and when I returned he commented, "Where is my bride?" referring to his wife for over 62-years of marriage. As I looked around she was only a couple of feet away across the room talking with relatives in a most engaged way which had come to be her strong suit. Her ear shot was close so of course she overhead the comment, and just as I met her glance, she smiled. She never missed a beat with the conversation she was fully engaged in, but I sensed something registered with her; the chemistry they two shared was undeniable and powerful, genuine and seemly had withstood the test of time. He, after all the years, still referred to her as "my bride" and it held special meaning between the two. A true love that stood the test of time, someone who would adore their partner and the relationship. It was what I wanted too.

In retrospect, when I think back on all the family weekend outings and vacations my family shared with my aunt and uncle over the years, I suspect all my perceptions on how relationships are supposed to be were unknowingly formed by observing their relationship.

This was my healthy template of how relationships were supposed to be. In many respects I am grateful and in other ways I am reminded by my own relationships of how difficult it is to sustain this level of appreciation over time. In my own relationships it has been difficult to express and maintain this level of appreciation for my partner in spite of the disagreements I faced with my husband. When you are in the mist of a committed relationship, it is impossible to predict how you will respond to disappointment, unmet needs, or the challenges of keeping the relationship novel and exciting over time. I learned it takes one person confident in their ability to give pleasure to another. A leap of faith that carries no guarantee.

To sustain what my aunt and uncle maintained over the years, I learned would take something well beyond trust of their mate so widely advocated in all the literature I have been exposed to, but would involve matters of risk and reciprocated mature reassurance. It takes courage to love unconditionally and this love is not always reciprocated even if you do not have any expectations, but when you know your mate is for you, you risk and that risk is accepted and reciprocated may be the greatest gift a person can give to another. My aunt Opal died in 2007 surrounded by loving friends after having lived a full life of giving herself unconditionally to a loving husband and family. I must believe her life had meaning, and hope it ended with no regrets.

The Consequences Of Seduction

All my life I had this fantasy of what I wanted, and any relationship that did not have the qualities to make this a reality for me would be quickly cast aside. I would not invest anything in them, or I would manipulate them so my suitor would fall madly in love with me. It was not until I met my match. He loved me unconditionally then cast me aside and it was only then that I felt the depths of agony. A painful pit of despair only the feelings of love lost can provide. Devine Karma some would call it. Read any good seduction *how to* manual and you too can be an expert at learning how to make other's fall madly in love with you. The *Art of Seduction* has been fine tuned to a science. It is a craft of sorts not for the faint of heart, but a quest, and desire to lay seize on a target of ones desire. It is a dangerous game many play with costly consequences.

Many may say they are not interested in such games of seduction, or it is evil and not for them, but we are intrigued and captivated by its effect. The person who practices *The Art of Seduction* becomes so intoxicated to participate in its practices ultimately become more experienced lovers. We all participate in a form of seduction to subdue a partner rather we want to admit it or not. The question is do you have the wherewithal to give of yourself to another regardless of what you stand to benefit in the long run. We are all searching for something outside of ourselves and this takes effort from one individual dedicating himself or herself to something that has the potential to give far more than their initial efforts.

Is love real? Can we really count on it to make us happy? What is the best way to recover from a devastating loss of affection? Do the emotional effects of experiencing a relationship loss make us stronger?

Should a person ever attempt to recapture what has been tampered with if a relationship becomes strained? Can people ever really repair broken relationships? What growth is possible after experiencing pain in relationships?

There is beauty in finding someone to love. I see beauty in a person's ability to admire their partner and display it to the world. The actual struggle a person will go through to show the world their perception of what they see in the other person that they love. To help the world see through their eyes what perceptions of the special qualities their partner has, as they view it, is enduring. It is admiration and appreciation.

Love is a verb. The actions you take to show your love. It starts with a commitment many say *yes* to. This is a basic willingness to verbally express to ones partner how they feel about them and what they appreciate. If a person is unable to explain what they desire from the relationship I would be wary. Typically people have a clear idea of what they are expecting to get out of a relationship long before they enter into it. Be it a short term, cordial, companion type relationship, or be it prospecting for a long term mate for matrimonial considerations. Then there are those who are looking for something in between with far less commitment involved compared to a short term relationship called friends with benefits, or no strings attached. In this arrangement, the relationship is more of a liaison. The cordiality of referring to one another by name is typically not necessary or important as too much over familiarity would only get in the way of moving on to the next liaison, or affair.

Expressing ones level of commitment in relationships reassures a partner of their love and commitment to one another. In a committed relationship, marriage, or common law partnerships, it never hurts to tell a partner that you love him or her and that you will always be there to foster trust.

In less committed relationships, this may be more difficult due to undefined goals for the relationship, distrust, even fear, and can create stress triggered by a preoccupation of negative thoughts, uncertainty, a perception of equality in the relationship, or worse fear of not having feelings reciprocated can all make the relationship meet an early demise. Now, a liaison is not to be judged by outsiders. People are free to direct their own lives and the type of attachments they wish to form. Those who enter into this form of relationship however it is highly recommended one have the courage not to keep the arrangement a secret from their partner. Being honest about the arrangement will allow the other person to make an informed decision about the direction they wish to go in the arrangement. It is only fair. A common courtesy as it were, to prevent delusional attachments and later hurt feelings. Moreover, several people would be more than willing to enter into this type of engagement and accept the stipulations set gladly.

In all my studies over a great deal of time striving to discover the true nature of relationships, I have discovered that an expert in the field of Couples Therapy is someone who has made the greatest amount of mistakes within a narrow field of study. The author included. Life can be a series of trail and errors so if at first you do not succeed in the relationships you pursue, know that maturity and time are the great equalizers. Ultimately, individuals arrive at a place where they are capable of sustaining mature relationships just by adopting greater awareness of what they want to avoid, what they desire most, then pursuing it. Also, know individuals achieve maturity in relationships by adopting increased self esteem, confidence with intimacy, exploring sexual boundaries, and a willingness to risk. It is this author's assertion that almost anyone can risk if they see a benefit to doing so and this chapter will continue to outline the necessary steps to gain just that.

Fear and Reluctance

In Couples Therapy, a popular dynamics processed is the theme of fear while the other is reluctant to give more of themselves for fear of rejection. One inevitability begins to pull away emotionally from their partner out of fear their partner will not be able to meet their individual needs. So as a result, one elects to only give as much as the other. The other partner is willing to be open in the relationship, but decides their level of intimacy shared will be based on their partner's level of giving. A modern day Tit for Tate dynamics.

One partner tells themselves they are too afraid to take a risk with their partner, and unwilling to seek out another relationship in which their needs can be met with someone who appreciates them. The dilemma is "I desire a relationship and I am unwilling to be intimate with my partner." You can never have both as it is a dilemma in which you must choose one choice over the other choice. Better sooner then later.

Let us look at the risks. If in this example a person finds themselves in a relationship where they are too fearful to allow themselves to be vulnerable, the other partner will never be given the opportunity to know their partner fully. We risk not being known and we risk opportunities for greater intimacy in the relationship. To be known is the pathway to greater trust to be shared that allows for the explicit expressions of that which we desire most. If we keep this valuable piece of information hidden, it will almost ensure that no one will be able to satisfy your needs because you have limited the other's ability to take action in areas that will satisfy you. In part, what this equates to is those areas that could be most satisfied by another remain unidentified.

The implicit message is you are hesitant about the relationship. People tend to pursue others who do not have an adverse reaction to them as individuals. The perception of another's acceptance has powerful emotional consequences. To not take risks and allow ourselves to be vulnerable is what prevents people from self confronting how they feel about themselves. At the core each person has a undeniable vulnerability tied to some form of pain and if discovered many believe it will make them susceptible to manipulation, or will place them at risk of being rejected because of the nature of the vulnerability. On the contrary, it is what makes us more attractive to others. Perfection is boring. Everyone has imperfections, just different ones. Moreover, anyone who attempts to conceal pain, or appears unaffected by life's pain, is ambivalent because feeling anything would become overwhelming. The ambivalent person lacks passion and this is neither seductive nor attractive. The inner struggle to reveal themselves, or not, and what this would mean, is why we experience anxiety.

To be known means a person is willing to express fully how they feel about their partner. Fully expressing what is working and what needs are not being met, expressing what they love about their mate, and what they desire to experience more of in the relationship. And, after these concerns and desires have been expressed, continues to be willing to satisfy their mate's desires, in addition to expressing what they appreciate and would do anything to maintain what they have together is being known. In doing so, the partner becomes known by the other.

If a person is in a relationship and has convinced themselves their needs are not being met, has lost all enthusiasm to stand up for themselves, resigns to having a less than satisfying relationship what results is the two can become reactive to one another. Arguments increase as well as the amount and scope of conflicts, or they ignore and avoid all contact yet remain fused in an unhealthy relationship. Couples in this predicament deserve better. They deserve to give themselves the benefit of exercising a sense of maturity in the relationship by tackling the conflicts head on despite uncertainties that exist. When executed properly, individuals typically come to a place of maturity where they can see for themselves making choices to stay in an unsatisfying relationship because they have convinced themselves no one else will value what they have to offer, is self defeating, and becomes frustrating for most to settle for this type of lower grade relationship.

In essence, the person that settles in any relationship is telling themselves *I don't like my relationship* and *I would rather be sad* instead of directing individual efforts towards a better relationship that has greater potential to make them happy. *I will just continue with something unsatisfying* and complain about it. As we get to understand this couple's dilemma, we find that both are committed to the relationship and appreciate one another, which could be easily overlooked.

I am not recommending people leave relationships prematurely if they are not working. Only leave a relationship after you have used it to grow yourself up. The growth and knowledge you gain from this relationship will only help you in establishing a more mature relationship with your next partner if a person decides leaving the relationship is what would be best, but often it is not. The choice in favor of personal growth over pain, is to stick it out and address the conflicting dilemma before reaching any conclusion. Furthermore, do not make the assumption that in this dynamics one partner may be more mature than the other to explain the dilemma. Both are of similar maturity levels. We all couple up, and marry at the same level of differentiation and maturity level.

If you can see the dynamics in this example you are right on point and can probably imagine how the story will end for a couple in this predicament. Poorly if one does not decide in advance the direction they would like the relationship to go. One becomes frustrated that the other has become selfish, unreasonable, perhaps harbors several complaints about what the other is not doing. One partner may even offer unsolicited negative comments to the other as a loving reminder of what the other is not doing, or make unsolicited negative comments on how one partner's efforts to make them happy *just misses the mark* of their expectations and offers no solution, just criticism. In a typical Couples Therapy session after I have assessed the depth of the dilemma and level of commitment each has for one another, I will ask, *What would it take for you to give first in the relationship?*

The wife says, *Well I would have to trust my needs would be met too.*

Remember maturity is not always defined by age when it comes to relationships in my personal understanding, my professional experience, as well as experiences with my own intimate relationships. Not even ones level of professional accomplishments can make them untouched by the hardships common in all striving to obtain, or improve relationships. The satire of life can however offer valuable insights if we take the time to learn from what we observe.

Before we continue this chapter on relationships, I would like to ask the reader to think of a relationship you would like to improve and what it would take for you to make it so. Then, based on all responses you developed, answer if you are willing to do those things even if the other person does nothing?

If there is something you are waiting for, do it now.

Regret in Relationships

In moments of grief and loss we can easily translate familiar scenes played out in hospitals as they are universal and often does not require language to understand the depth of ones loss. We instinctually understand the situation, or do we.

He sat at the conference room table attempting to mask his tears, but they did not go unnoticed by the funeral director. He says, "you must have loved your father very much." He cries softly feeling comforted in his moment of tremendous grief. In that moment though, it was the realization of not having known his father at all in the brief time he was alive. During his life the barriers had been kept too high, the distance too great. This clarity gained through the experience of grief and loss triggered a unique sense of mature awareness never pondered before confirming that having been granted the gift of more time with his father, he questioned to himself if more of the same would be the result.

Under these situations of finality, we question our connections to others when we experience grief so great the realization of unmet needs is all that remains in the moment. The person is left with only time to reflect on what is really lost beyond the selfish feelings that typically surface in times of need. We question if given more time to have made the situation repairable; would lessen our grief. We may even attempt to analyze our actions in opportunities that presented themselves in the past, lost, could had been handled differently if recaptured.

To question silently if there would have been more time would the relationship been closer, or would the two have just settled for a low grade level of closeness like what had become so comfortable in all the years prior. It was the years of neglected needs which prevent most from reaching out first when opportunities present themselves. To ponder what decisions were made to harm intentionally those one loves. Becoming aware of this in retrospect, brings the greatest sorrow. In retrospect, it is a form of sadistic revenge that translates into a continued sense of being hurt. The question then becomes, knowing what we know now, would we make the same decisions? Factor in a new respect for time and its consequences. Not only for the relationships they can not conceivably repair now, but those to come in the future. We cannot change what has already occurred, but perhaps take the mistakes of the past as learning opportunities to make future relationships better. This is growth. The next similar opportunity that presents itself will you do something different in the moment regardless of the outcome, or anxiety felt?

Despite the uncertainty we feel when we risk in relationships; we can find the courage to act. Be decisive. Be deliberate in ones actions towards others. Decide no longer to want to settle for less than a quality relationship. We can give ourselves permission to be more accepting of others. This does not mean we have to pacify others or deny our own needs, but rather take more responsibility in our relationships because relationships design themselves by the degree of personal disclosure and boundaries each supplies.

Superficial Versus Intimate Relationships

Relationships are a normal part of daily life. We have different types of relationships by default of our busy lives and all the people we must interact with to conduct the business of daily living. For example over time of shopping at the same food mart, we develop a familiar relationship with our butcher, or with the cashier who eagerly tallies your groceries on each visit. We develop relationships with coworkers, and family members. And, perhaps the neighbor who never appears to have any visitors except you, but eagerly invites you in with an enticing offer you cannot refuse. Each can be categorized by the depth of intimacy we have in those relationships. Some are more superficial than others, and some relationships you have will be very intimate. Intimacy means within. It refers to a relationship that allows another person to cross the normal boundaries of defensiveness and enter into that space where we are our most authentic self.

In Psychology, to maintain good Mental Health, it is important to be authentic in all our relationships and to become aware to limit those relationships that do not allow us to be congruent. It can cause undue stress and conflict when people are not allowed to be themselves lets say at work, and then when at home are perceived differently. Although most of us desperately want intimacy, at the same time we fear it. The risk in intimate communication is that the other might not accept us after we have shared our deepest feelings. But, the alternative is experiencing aloneness or feeling the failure of knowing another's love or deep respect when it does exist and had been offered.

Communication is the key to intimacy, for it is only through the exchange of meaning and the sharing of feelings that deep understanding and Psychological closeness can be achieved. Of course, the meaning shared is of a special kind. Intimate communication occurs when a friend opens his heart to you in such a way that you are encouraged to come out from behind your mask of vulnerability and into a fresh experience of mutual understanding. In this experience, we are more open, more ready for positive growth, more loving and more alive.

Intimacy is not necessarily sexual. In fact, sexual relationships might not be intimate at all except in a purely physical sense. Intimacy can exist between parents and children, husband and wife, brothers and sisters. It is experienced among friends, relatives, and even business partners. When intimacy develops, we experience a sense of relatedness, belonging, and acceptance that is extremely satisfying. To enter into a quality relationship is the single most consequential goal for most, and can be the most painful experience we will ever endure. If you have never experienced the dread of lost love, you will. Everyone does at least once in a lifetime if you live long enough and have the courage to risk in your relationships. If you can muster the courage to love others, I wish you the beauty of pure acceptance that comes from experiencing love many times in your lifetime. Love more than once despite the pain that ensues. It is worth the risk. Allow others to give witness to your life and all the unique gifts you have to contribute.

Ms. Cloé Madanes, Family Therapist, author of *Strategic Family Therapy* (1981), advocates a theory of social action and has shared projects with Mr. Anthony Robbins, a world renowned author and Peak Performance speaker to his credit. Ms. Madanes outlines a core belief that there are six universal human needs that can be satisfied in positive or negative ways. They are Security, Variety, Love and Connection, Significance, Growth, and Contribution.

The first four *universal human needs* are essential to human survival, she contends. The last two are essential to human fulfillment. Ultimately, she explains that no one person, even if in a committed relationship cannot be expected to fulfill all these needs for another. When couples have needs which are different from one another or are in conflict, people will look at how they can get their needs met that are socially acceptable. If one partner attempts to meet two of their partner's needs a genuine connection can be formed and the other four unmet needs will be sought after in other ways, outside the relationship, that the person initiates that are healthy and socially acceptable. However if a partner strives to satisfy four or more basic needs for another person, this can be unhealthy in relationships and is considered a form of addiction, according to Ms. Madanes based on a live seminar this author attended and participated in while completing Doctoral studies at Alliant International University, Los Angeles, California, 2004.

Thankfully, I have risked beyond the conceivable to obtain that which could have never been mine alone. Yet still, I risked. When one is willing to give beyond their set boundaries for the sake of love, this is the breaking point where we begin to self reflect, and it is the most important phase in ones life we allow ourselves the opportunity to gain clarity. Define that which we value most. Unfortunately, this phase is seldom contemplated in moments of contentment.

When we are happy, we rarely give much energy to matters of what would make it even more enjoyable because we are so happy in the moment. When we enter into tough and challenging times this is when most will reflect because they have reached a threshold of becoming uncomfortable they desire an escape from. The tough times are typically painful, but in this period of pain, it motivates us individually to change the situation. Therefore, pain is *always necessary* to achieve Psychological Growth. We cannot be expected to be perfect as alluded to above. Striving to be perfect hinders our ability to acknowledge when we are feeling uncomfortable thus impedes opportunities for deep contemplation that can only occur in adversity leading to growth.

Unconditional Love

This perception that unconditional love is the best quality to put forth in ones relationships is a common shared belief and behavior many subscribe to. Sometimes it leaves you with poor results when the object of your desire does not reciprocate, and sometimes you are left with an incredibly satisfying relationship most would be envious of. When we speak of unconditional love most naturally think of how it is applied externally. Or, the consequences of taking such leaps of faith towards another or the vulnerability one would become susceptible to.

An alternative perspective states if a person has self love, sharing this with another has tremendous mutual benefits. The understanding is individuals can choose to mentally surrender to their inner critic and continue to love themselves unconditionally. What they then choose to give away to another never subtracts from what they are, or what we have to give. To love others as they *love and accept themselves unconditionally* is the core foundation of all those who possess a confident loving core of well being. Ultimately, they have more to give away to others and this never subtracts from their core. It is also true within the *Laws of Attraction* what we extend to others is returned in subtle ways, and placing conditions on what we expect only intensifies in relationship with others.

Achieving the best relationship you desire is never a sure thing. It is a gamble and there is no wrong way to proceed. It is just important that you allow yourself to experience the process of being in a relationship. The experience is the best teacher. Within this process we have an opportunity to learn about ourselves, redefine our values and preferences, and to become more proficient at the art of mastering our anxieties when conflicts surface. It is just the nature of the dance in relationships. If you are willing to risk and your relationship ends abruptly, an opportunity exists for you to become stronger in your next relationship by obtaining clarity surrounding the type of relationship you desire.

Proven Strategies To Improve Relationships

Many miss the mark by not making their intimate relationships priority. Relationships take work. Do the hard work, meaning you take time for your partner and ensure there are opportunities to spend quality time together. It has often been repeated here, Love is a verb. It is something you do. The actions you take, the attitude you express, the extent of behavioral actions taken and efforts extended towards another to make a partner happy and feel appreciated will serve you beyond measure to foster increased intimacy. Only trust in believing this perspective is a true belief will encourage future behavioral actions and intent. Remember the simple phrase: If your partner is happy, you will be happy as you receive the benefits of their appreciation you have extended.

The most important questions to ask one self in relationships has been documented, and has been proven over time. Evidence this is true stems from experience caring for the elderly. I began to notice a pattern of what patients would talk about as they weathered through their final days. I learned that most individuals before dying ask themselves two important questions: Who loves me? And, who did I allow to love me? I know this for sure that many who lie pondering the last moments in this life, these two questions have been documented as the single most important questions all humans ask before dying regardless of race, culture, age, economic status, the amount of children they may have had, or not had. Some may have had children yet we all know this is not a given people actually are guaranteed their children's devoted love in the end. People are predictable. Both in their capacity to disappoint another beyond belief, as well as in their capacity to surpass our expectations. The challenge is always to choose having a firm foundational core within self to give first that which we desire most from others. The only guarantee one truly has is to love others unconditionally. Those who appreciate what you have to offer will surface and give to you beyond measure. This is the nature of love. We can only front load our options in life. Give unconditionally expecting noting in return and hope for a return much later down the road. Never demand love. Just live by the values you commit to in this lifetime and you will be rewarded in the end by your selfless efforts extended to others.

What you can do to improve your relationships now include the following strategies.

1. Give first unconditionally

2. Trust the process

3. Contribute to the process

4. Be loving yourself if what you want is love

5. In order to be capable of receiving love you must always give what it is you want to receive. In life, you never get more than you are willing to give.

6. Be the person you wish to attract

7. Never ask your partner to be more than you are willing to be for yourself!

8. Allow yourself to be vulnerable

9. Talk with your partner openly and honestly

10. Discuss the difficult topics even if you stand to risk rejection. Knowing where you stand in the relationship is always a more powerful position to have than standing in the wings waiting for the day you both discover you have reached a deal breaker. Listen, you deserve to have what you want now. Not ten years from now because you were too fearful to go after it now.

11. Don't sacrifice yourself for the relationship

12. Have a vested interest in your own projects. The projects that inspire you and make you a more interesting and engaging passionate person. And, have projects, or interests, you can share together with a partner.

13. Have confidence! Just because it is incredibly attractive and seductive.

14. Take responsibility for your feelings

15. Know you can only change yourself. Accept your partner as they are. If you notice how difficult it is for you to change think about the amount of manipulation you will have to put forth to have someone else change just to suit you. It is not fair in any relationship. Plus, if we demand your partner change to suit you, and they do, we typically grow to resent them for giving in to our wishes and come to see them as weak. It is not rational, but it is what we do. It is easier to just change ourselves.

16. Let go of absolute value judgments

17. Be yourself always. No excuses! Let other's ponder why they do not have the guts to live more authentically.

18. Know your intentions behind your words

19. Communicate your wants and needs to your partner. Appreciate what a partner is *willing to give* within their comfort level.

20. Drop your expectations of how your mate should be

21. When a partner shows you who they really are the first time believe them. This is likely their true self and it is easier to find a partner who shares your values than attempting to change them to suit your values.

22. Listen with your whole body, mind, soul, instincts, when choosing a compatible partner. Do not sell yourself short. Life is too short to miss out on what you deserve and desire.

23. Express your appreciation and gratitude openly and often

24. Examine your beliefs about love & relationships

25. Have a dialogue about your beliefs, and expectations in a relationship

26. Use humor to defuse difficult situations and conflicts, but never avoid feeling the anxiety that surfaces as this is an indicator something must be explored more in depth for growth

27. Examine your desire to control your partner

28. Say *Yes* more often to positive opportunities

Being Able To Direct Ones Own Life

A Differentiated Based Approach encourages and motivates people to be able to direct one's own life. People who can not do this are afraid because they do not know what they truly want. Another's needs may be more important than their own subsequently a person may become unduly influenced and subject to engage in negative or risky activities simply because the other person wants to.

KEY: When we change, we expect others around us to change also. They rarely do though and remain the same.

GROWTH: To do something different from the family you were brought up with and staying connected to one's significant other.

THE MAJOR TASK:
(1) The ability to get close and express warmth with loved ones.
(2) How can you get up close with an intimate partner in ways you have not previously?
(3) Share self not boundaries.
(4) Share personal experiences, thoughts of what you are apprehensive about, fears, and/or what you are looking forward to.

The Rules of Relationships

Don't change a thing I want to respect you!

There are just a few rules to consider when entering into a quality relationship. First, expectations must remain realistic and kept at a minimum. Secondly, remember that all relationships require maturity. Third, consider your intimate relationships as your last opportunity to grow yourself up. In a committed relationship, never expect the other person to change because they will not. If they do change, you will think they are weak and learn to despise them. If they do not change and stay the same, you will grow to resent them. It is easier to change ones self.

The test question for any relationship to measure ones openness, vulnerabilities, or defenses is to ask them about their childhood experiences as more trust is gained in the relationship. You may even inquire about the level of intimacy there was between their parents, and siblings. A more direct approach is to inquire if they were loved as a child. Their initial response without the filter of defensiveness, or attempts to mask the truth will provide you with all the evidence you need to predict the quality of relationship they may feel most comfortable in as an adult. Another direct question to ask those who have had a serious relationship or marriage is if they feel they married the wrong person. It is too personal for most and triggers a normal level of defensiveness yet we are curious about their potential responses.

If you are age 73 and can respond I married the love of my life, you have lived a full life indeed and perhaps were luckier than most. But really love is not for the lucky it is for all of us if we are willing to be mature enough to seek out relationships and do the necessary work to maintain them over time.

Gaining a sense of ones early intimate experiences can allow us a glimpse into the depth of what another may be capable of providing emotionally. If they have never felt love, it may be a struggle to penetrate the emotional barriers. This may either be similar to your own experiences, or it may be a drastic difference from your early experiences. Either case it is good to play on one another's strengths and weakness to support ones partner. And, sometimes people pursue love so passionately; that which they long for, because they were never provided it in childhood.

Achieving greater maturity also means we take full responsibility for ourselves and do not assume it is another's responsibility. If parents have not fostered a sense of independence in their children, the adult will just look to their partner to take care of them, or attaching to best friends to assist with personal responsibilities which is often perceived as an unhealthy level of dependence on others to meet our personal unmet needs.

PART IV:

THE PRÉCIPICE

CHAPTER NINE

The Précipice

*T*he précipice in relationships is a defining moment. It is a crucial defining moment when a person has to decide what direction they will go next. Ponder for once and for all which relationship is most important. The relationships with self, or others? To relinquish the needs of self to receive something of more value despite possible consequences of immense pain and suffering, or to deny oneself of pleasure.

Imagine standing on a steep cliff, as far as the eye can see is the most amazing view of surreal nature frozen there in that very moment in all its perfection. There you are. Images from your past of perfect examples you have used as reference for your concept of nature and beauty come to mind. This intellectual engagement is unconscious; you have no control over it. We need a starting reference point to help us understand and make sense of what we are processing visually and emotionally. Nature, it registers, and then we can proceed. Images may conjure up emotional states of relaxation, feeling calm and feelings of harmony. Feeling reflective perhaps stirred up by the lack of ambient noise distractions. The calmness allows your muscles to relax as if a steady stream of light white mist is gently swaging through you.

There you are atop a steep overhanging mountainous cliff. In this very moment, the metaphorical explorer has limited choices to choose. Really there are only four choices; they can go forward off the cliff and face a long plunge into self destruction, go sideways on the cliff going neither backwards or forward and experience the same path again, stay still in the spot they are in to further ponder their reflective state of being stuck, or visualize removing oneself from the cliff and experience something new. Take a challenge; risk.

The fourth choice is to allow oneself to explore something new by self confronting their character. The strength in this is becoming more differentiated and compelling beyond measure. It is uniquely yours alone, yet more difficult to initiate or to experience on ones own without a dilemma to match it against. You see the metaphorical explorer may find it difficult to make the best decision unless ones choice has significant consequences.

It is as if the explorer must have clarity of thought in order to make an informed decision and possess certainty about the direction he wants to go before proceeding forward from this spot on the cliff.

Sure, an explorer could find himself on a high cliff and stay there all night pondering his choices, or what his next step should be, but as night falls, it will become uncomfortable for the explorer. Time is wasted. The person becomes stagnant. Let's face it this is not an attractive place to find oneself as it only attracts needy less confident people in our life. Or worst, the need for rescuing becomes dominate in thought; dependent on someone else to force a choice and take control over the current situation.

We must all make our own individual decisions for ourselves, for better or worse, there is no escape from this individual responsibility we have to make definitive decisions that have the potential to change the course of our lives as we know it. The choices must be made with such certainty of thought because once a decision is made, reversing it is always attached with such influence over other matters we must be confident in the effect they will have. For better or worst, be able to adapt to whatever fall out our decisions will manifest later for all those involved therefore it is wise to consider likely consequences of our decisions first.

In the movie *The Edge* starring Anthony Hopkins, written by David Mamet, Director Lee Tamahori, one of the lines in the movie states *You know why people die in the woods? They die of shame.*

If ever lost in the woods, could you survive? If ever personally faced with insurmountable odds of defeat, life, or death dilemmas, new situations you must navigate and having no reference points to draw upon, how would you navigate them? How would you fare? The movie inadvertently moves the viewer to question *How* do you usually face new challenges?

It's easy to respond to these difficult questions, just look at your last big obstacle. Did you face it full on, or did you shriek from the challenge that you faced? Did you question first *How did I get into this?* then become overwhelmed, fearful, or worst afraid to admit you had gotten yourself in such a predicament? Not admitting difficult situations to ourselves, or others only delays receiving help. This line of questioning contemplating their current state can also serve as a means to procrastinate and further avoid a situation until the problem becomes larger and increasingly unmanageable.

This is the stuff of life we all face. It's the normalcy we all face. Moreover, taking the steps to turn it all around takes courage. To be deliberate and decisive regardless of its effects because we have stood true to our character and drive to meet our overriding goals towards fulfillment as difficult for most to commit to.

Shame is a painful emotion caused by a strong sense of guilt, embarrassment, feelings of inadequacy, unworthiness, or disgrace one feels that is brought upon by dishonor or feeling great disappointment. The type of shame that comes from seeing an opportunity, yet lacking the passion or inner strength to really go for it full on.

In *The Edge*, the obstacle was to conquer a larger than life Black Bear in the great wild outdoors of an unexplored region of Alaska. The plot scenario writer David Mamet creates is of a young gorgeous female model often viewed as engaged with her rich billionaire husband Charles, played by Anthony Hopkins. A much younger male and fashion photographer, Robert Green, played by Alec Baldwin, enters into the scenario to complicate matters and to provide his model with additional outlets for satisfying her lust for pleasure. Robert Green, the photographer, in the scenario is ultimately however taken beyond his capacity for survival.

The character Robert Green matched against Charles, initially believes he has the upper hand. When their plane crashes in the middle of uncharted Alaska, a strong mind game erupts between the jealous husband and the younger photographer as they attempt to get back to civilization. To survive in the wilderness full of man-killing bears they need each other, but the smarter of the two men Charles, is suspicious that Robert is having an affair with his wife.

Charles elects early on to put their current adulterous dilemmas aside for the greater good of basic survival and ultimately when Charles is faced with the opportunity to slay his opponent the fashion photographer, Charles makes several calculated courageous decisive actions that will save them both if they work together. Ultimately, the fashion photographer dies, but not by Charles' actions, from a life sustaining injury just at the moment the rescue sea plane arrives at the remote Alaskan shore bank. This crucial scene speaks to Charles's commitment to change in the moment. What lies before Charles is a moment of clarity to do things differently. He finds new hope for pursuing matters left undone, adventures he had planned for but were seen as unachievable became then, now viewed as within his reach.

It is a wonderful metaphor for all of life's great obstacles. The explorer, when placed into a life or death struggle to survive, his true character is tested and must navigate something never attempted before. It is a test of will and the measure of ones level of perseverance. The movie urges the viewer to contemplate what obstacles they face, and how much courage, creatively, and passion to survive over obstacles they the individual is willing to put forth to save themselves. In this author's personal opinion, Charles chooses goodness to prevail in his decision to be compassionate towards Robert Green above and beyond their conflicts.

One character breaks down under the pressure and displays fear. He doubts his strength, questions if he can muster up the wherewithal to slay the bear when his life is at stake. Have you ever been in a situation where you had to make a decision where there were only two choices? Live or die? Presented with a dilemma you must choose between changing the course of your life to live with fulfillment or to settle into a life of mediocrity based on self-imposed fears?

One choice gives you greater freedom and fulfillment in the long run, and the other choice offered, death or dissatisfaction by not taking action? We are faced by these dilemmas and still many fail to take action on important decisions knowing the consequences of not taking action will substantially impact ones livelihood negatively. It is what we do as humans. We fail to make the difficult decisions when change is most called for. Either we fail to see the big picture or we fail to take action when it matters most because we have not yet learned that all in life is a learning curve. The more chances we take in life give us a greater advantage to gain greater proficiency and expertise over difficult tasks. With more difficult opportunities to experience success, the greater our confidence levels raise so later ultimately we can face difficult tasks knowing we have the ability to concur even the most difficult tasks and become resilient to tackle even the impossible. I hope your life will never call for the conquering of bear, but the same principles apply to day to day dilemmas.

In life, there will be several opportunities to let oneself down by not living up to your expectations, or the expectations of others. What then becomes crucial is ones ability to adapt. To thrive in ones environment regardless of obstacles presented. The stuff of greatness is to understand one principle I have learned thus far. Life is difficult and there will always be a fair amount of loss and pain we must all endure to appreciate life more fully. No matter what happens, you will always have decisions to make about the direction of your life. Know that in life no one person other than yourself can really make these decisions for you and through it all will require a display of deliberate courage on your part.

> *If you can't find the drama in everyday life, you are not living!*
>
> Robert McKee

Life is occurring all around us everyday. Most make the mistake of searching for something outside of themselves to find the cure-all to life's dilemmas when in fact if we just slow down enough to examine what is there, and how we experience it, answers become clear as to how one can live a more fulfilling life and the choices we must make to achieve happiness. Often the greatest obstacles presented is we want to make decisions that will have low impact, not stir things up too much, but this is not possible. All choices will have great impact over ones life path and will affect all those around you.

Think back on a relationship in which a dilemma surfaced. Remember a situation that surfaced in your current relationship, or a past relationship, in which there was significant conflict. A deal breaker that surfaced that there seemed to be no escape. For example, you enter into a relationship with full knowledge your mate prefers you, and then the dynamics of the relationship began to change. Your partner's obsession towards other outside activities suddenly interferes with the quality and amount of time spent together as a couple. It can be the mildly innocent infatuation with a coworker, or the over involvement with other activities such as pursuing greed, addictions, lust, all interfering with the closeness you once shared. In some cases, it can be the sudden awareness that abusive tendencies have begun to surface in the relationship. Or, there is an awareness of an abusive intentional need to degrade ones partner to feel better about themselves to achieve control and power over another. Perhaps it is the acknowledgment ones partner is no longer sexually satisfying. The deal breakers which seemly appear to have more impact, but are difficult to address verbally and to resolve without creating additional conflicts.

The moment someone changes, or veers away from the original plan, the relationship dynamics change. We can either accept those changes and continue with the relationship status quo with full knowledge something significant has changed and this is not *What I barged for* and accept the new direction in the relationship, or they can waste time pondering if this new direction is what one desires too. Chances are it is not. Conflict is an opportunity to ponder more deeply when a dilemma is created.

We Begin To Evaluate What Is Occurring In A Relationship

All the situations described here are reversible if addressed. Often the choices a person comes up with seem too difficult, overwhelming, or require extreme effort they don't feel in the moment they are presently capable of accomplishing, so they continue to tell themselves I'm stuck, or fresh out of options when in fact this is a lie. They know exactly what to do, just not willing to take action. If you fall in this boat you are not alone, everyone does it. Or, you may fall into the trap of standing up for yourself, confronting what situations are disagreeable in the relationship, even terminating the relationship, but then find yourself repeating the same mistakes in your next relationship. It is easy to blame others for our horrible predicaments. We take our anguish out on others and convince ourselves how good a person we are as a default way of letting ourselves off the hook for our actions not taken.

Second Acts

John F. Fitzgerald was once quoted as saying *There are no second acts in American lives.* Over time I have come to disagree with his observations. In reality, we see *second acts* occurring all the time. For example, when a fifty-year marriage takes a sudden divergence from the comfort of day-to-day reliance on one another. One dies, and the other spouse has to begin again. Or, one begins to display signs of Dementia and nuances in the relationship change; one partner has to expect different responses from a now unresponsive mate. This is a sad thought to contemplate, but is more common in the every day lives of many.

When you are in the midst of contemplating a big decision that will change everything, as you know it, then what? Is this not a chance to do things differently? Might this be viewed as an opportunity to show a different side of yourself? We can decide to show-up fully with every fiber of your existence, face the fear, or to shrink under the pressure. Either way we choose or our life dynamics does not allow us the full insight of our choices.

We humans, granted enormous opportunities in life, and are equally wealthy in our ability to take total control over the direction of our lives. We can make one decision that has the potential to change everything around, or we allow our opportunities to get the best of us. In keeping with this line of thought if what we seek is lasting fulfillment, which is not gained by keeping things the same; we have no alternative but to make different choices for ourselves.

Your metaphorical audience, those who have taken an interest in you as witness of your life direction, braces itself on the edge of their seat waiting to see how the story will end. The audience always longs for a glimpse of how the story will unfold. What happens next? What unforeseen directions the story will take leading the character down different directions most in keeping with their true character. The audience waits to see what choices the character will make that are most unexpected and uplifting.

The now famous author Mr. Fitzgerald may have been referring to the finality of life as in death when he said there are no *Second Acts,* but this author would like to believe that while we are living there are opportunities over the course of a lifetime for *Second Acts.* If we as unique individuals allow ourselves to passionately move forward and take full advantage of opportunities presented, individuals can allow themselves even in moments of uncertainty, to achieve fulfillment beyond measure.

à Donf

REFERENCES

Akutagawa, Ryunosuke. (1972). Rashomon *and Other Stories.* Liveright Publishing Corporation.

American Psychiatric Association, (2000). *Diagnostic and Statistical Manual of Mental Disorders Text Revision (DSM-IV-TR),* Fourth Edition, American Psychiatric Association, Washington, DC.

Ayers, Michael, and Daniel Garber., (1998). *Cambridge History of Seventeenth-Century Philosophy.* Cambridge, U.K.

Barbara Sher, (1996). *Live the Life You Love.* New York Delacorte Press.

Boyle, M., (1990). *Schizophrenia: A Scientific Delusion?* London: Routledge Publishing.

Boyle, M., (2002). *Schizophrenia: A Scientific Delusion?* Second Edition. London: Routledge Publishing.

Campbell, J., (1949). *The Hero with a Thousand Faces.*

Campbell, J., (1959). The Masks of God.

Egan, G., (1971). *Encounter Groups: Basic Reading.* California: Brooks/Cole Publishing Company.

Fillingham, L. A. (1993). Foucault *For Beginners*. New York, NY: Writers and Readers Publishing, Inc.

Frankl, V., (1946). *Man's Search for Meaning*. Boston: Beacon Press.

Friedman, M., (1980). *Overcoming the Fear of Success*. New York, Warner Books.

Fromm, Erich, (1954). *The Psychology of Normalcy*. New York, NY.

Goffman, E., (1961). *Asylums Essays on the Social Situation of Mental Patients and Other Inmates*. Anchor Books Doubleday & Company, Inc., Garden City, New York.

Goldstein, J., (2003). *Sacred Wounds Succeeding Because Of Life's Pain*. Harper Collins Publishers, Inc., New York, NY.

Gottman, John, M., and DeClaire, J., (2001). *The Relationship Cure*. Three Rivers Press, New York, NY.

Gottschalk, L. A., Fronszek, J., & Buchsbaum, M., (1993). *The Cerebral Neurobiology of Hope and Hopelessness*. Psychiatry, 56.

Greene, Robert. (2001). The *Art of Seduction*. Viking Adult, Penguin Group Publishing, New York, NY.

Haas, Kurt, (1975). *Growth Encounter, A Guide for Groups*. Chicago: Nelson-Hall.

Kopp, Sheldon B. (1972). If *You Meet The Buddha On The Road, Kill Him! The Pilgrimage Of Psychotherapy Patients*.

Krishnamurti, J., (1996). *Total Freedom The Essential Krishnamurti*. Haper Collins Publishers, New York, NY.

Kubler-Ross, E., (1973). *On Death and Dying*, Routledge.

Kubler-Ross, E., (2005). *On Grief and Grieving: Finding the Meaning of Grief Through the Five Stages of Loss*, Simon & Schuster Ltd.

Lieberman, M., Yalom, I., Miles, M., (1973). *Encounter Groups.* First Facts. New York: Basic Books, Inc. Publishers.

Lofton, L. (2004) *Schizophrenia and Recovery*, Alliant International University, Los Angeles, CA.

Mankiewicz, Herman J., Welles, Orsen Director. (1941). *Citizen Kane.* Released by RKO Pictures.

Maslow, A. H., (1943). *A Theory of Human Motivation.* Psychological Review.

Maslow, A. H., (1970). *Motivation and Personality*, 2nd. ed., Harper & Row, New York, NY.

Maslow, A., (1962). Toward a Psychology of Being.

Maslow, A., (1954). *Motivation and Personality.*

Mousltakas, C., (1968). *Individuality and Encounter.* Massachusetts: Howard A. Doyle Publishing Company.

Peterson, Christopher and Seligman, Martin, (2004). *Character Strengths and Virtues: A Handbook and Classification.* Oxford University Press.

Scavio, M. J., Regas, S., (1997). *Historical Parallels in the Development of Physics and Psychology*, Second Edition, Kendall/Hunt Publishing Company, Dubuque, Iowa.

Schnarch, D., (1991). *Constructing the Sexual Crucible An Integration of Sexual and Marital Therapy.* W. W. Norton & Company, Inc., New York, NY.

Schnarch, D., (1997). *Passionate Marriage Love, Sex, and Intimacy in Emotionally Committed Relationships.* W. W. Norton & Company, New York, NY.

Schnarch, D., (2002). *Resurrecting Sex.* Harper Collins, New York, NY.

Seligman, Martin, (1990). *Learned Optimism: How to change your mind and your life.* Free Press.

Seligman, Martin, (2002). *Authentic Happiness: Using the New Positive Psychology to Realize Your Potential for Lasting Fulfillment.* Free Press.

Smith, P., (1980). *Small Groups and Personal Change.* London: Methuen.

Sorensen, J., Cudlipp, E., (1973). *The New Way To Become The Person You'd Like To Be.* New York: David McKay Company, Inc.

Southard, Samuel. (1974). Your *Guide To Group Experience.* New York and Nashville: Abingdon Press.

Sternberg, R. J. (1988) *The Triangle of Love: Intimacy, Passion, Commitment,* Basic Books (ISBN 0465087469).

Sternberg, R. J., (1986). *A Triangular Theory Of Love. Psychological Review.*

Sutherland, Stuart (1996). *The International Dictionary of Psychology,* Second Edition. The Crossroad Publishing Company, New York, NY.

Wahba, M. A., Bridwell, L. G., (1976). *Maslow reconsidered A review of research on the need hierarchy theory.* Organizational Behavior and Human Performance.

DISCLAIMER

The information, ideas, and suggestions in this book are not intended as a substitute for professional advice. Before following any suggestions contained in this book, you should consult your personal physician or Mental Health professional. Neither the author nor the publisher shall be liable or responsible for any loss or damage allegedly arising as a consequence of your use or application of any information or suggestions in this book.